Wednesdays *with* Wyndham

More Titles by the Author:

My Morning Cup

There's a Turkey at Your Door:
and other devotional thoughts

Prime Rib:
Exploring a Woman's Value and Purpose

Spiritual Leadership for Women

Understanding Goose:
For anyone who has felt different, rejected, or empty

Jacob's Journey

Fruity Tunes and the Adventures of Rotten Apple

Rosie and Opal: Finding Hope

The Helping Garden

When the Chicken Hits the Fan

An Aging Grace

Every Day is a New Chance

The View from Paul's Window:
Paul's Teachings on Women

Wednesdays *with* Wyndham

GODLY WISDOM FOR EVERYDAY LIFE

JEANIE SHAW

Wednesdays *with* Wyndham:
Godly Wisdom for Everyday Life
©2020 by Jeanie Shaw

All rights are reserved. No part of this book may be duplicated, copied, translated, reproduced, or stored mechanically, digitally, or electronically without specific, written permission of the author and publisher.

All Scripture quotations, unless indicated, are taken from the Holy Bible, New International Version (NIV), copyright © 2011 by Biblica, Inc. Used by permission. All rights reserved worldwide.

The "NIV" and "New International Version" trademarks are registered in the United States Patent Trademark Office by the International Bible Society. Use of either trademark requires the permission of the International Bible Society.

Printed in the United States of America

ISBN-13: 9798574462553
Morning Cup Press

Cover design: Charlene Glatkowski
Interior design: Thais Gloor
Front cover photo credit: Melissa Miller
Back cover photo credit: Susan Dollar

www.jeaniesjourneys.com

To the loving memory of Wyndham Shaw

CONTENTS

Foreword by Gordon Ferguson 11

Introduction 17

1. Wisdom Knows Where to Find Wisdom.................21
2. Wisdom Knows You are Still Who You Are 25
3. Wisdom Always Leads by Example 30
4. Wisdom Knows "Tentative" 33
5. Wisdom Digs Deeply in the Right Places 37
6. Wisdom Is a Utility Player 42
7. Wisdom Speaks Aptly 46
8. Wisdom Finds the High Road..................................49
9. Wisdom Knows that Love Involves Action 53
10. Wisdom Is Impartial 57
11. Wisdom Breaks Barriers 62
12. Wisdom Persuades and Is Persuadable 67
13. Wisdom Has Vision in Dark Times.........................72
14. Wisdom Brings a Calming Voice of Reason 76
15. Wisdom Keeps Showing Up 80
16. Wisdom Understands Buckets and Funnels............84
17. Wisdom Breaks Through..89
18. Wisdom Never Gives Up 94
19. Wisdom Loves to Fish..99

20. Wisdom Offers a Safe Place 103

21. Wisdom Brings Resolution 107

22. Wisdom Believes "Even If" 110

23. Wisdom Finds God's Presence 116

24. Wisdom Is "Whataburger" 119

25. Wisdom Knows a Secret 123

26. Wisdom Connects 127

27. Wisdom Is Mind Change 131

28. Wisdom Loves to Laugh 136

29. Wisdom Clings to the Rock 140

30. Wisdom Builds Faith While Expressing Love 144

31. Wisdom Brings Abiding Friendship 148

32. Wisdom Speaks with the End in Mind 153

33. Wisdom Lives Today 156

34. Wisdom Finds the End of Me 161

35. Wisdom Overlooks 165

36. Wisdom Knows "Busy's" Purpose 170

37. Wisdom Considers 174

38. Wisdom Throws a Pebble 177

39. Wisdom Treasures Time 182

40. Wisdom Is Being There 188

41. Wisdom Takes Risks 193

42. Wisdom Learns to Dance 197

43. Wisdom Sits 201

44. Wisdom Values the Dinner Table 205

45. Wisdom Builds Family 209

46. Wisdom Wears a Blue Robe 214

47. Wisdom Encourages 218
48. Wisdom Imparts Confidence from God 221
49. Wisdom Imparts Values 225
50. Wisdom Makes God Our Strength 229
51. Wisdom Finds Spiritual Heroes 233
52. Wisdom Trusts 238
53. Wisdom Passes the Torch 242
54. Wisdom Finds Hope 246
55. Wisdom Finishes Victoriously...............................251
56. Wisdom Writes New Chapters 257

FOREWORD
by Gordon Ferguson

Where to begin? This short volume is simply the best devotional book I have ever read, hands down. It rises above whatever I would rank second by a fair margin. I think of sermons that have made a difference in my life with God and with people, and what gave them that effect. They were those that enabled me to take away one application that changed me. In a similar way, each of Jeanie's chapters has distilled gems of wisdom (about wisdom) into bite-sized chunks that leave you full in spite of their brevity. She is quite a master at doing that, as you will see.

Some people might choose to look right over this book if they know the background of it. It was written by a wife during the last several years of her husband's life as he was dying with a debilitating illness. You might think it's a gushy mess of emotions being poured out in all directions. Maybe it's merely grief put into print as a way of trying to work through it. Maybe it's an attempt to deny the inevitable realities by painting a happy face through words. Maybe if you are male, you have an underlying sense (perhaps subconsciously) that a woman writer would make it difficult or impossible for you to connect with her. Maybe, maybe, maybe.

Wrong, wrong, wrong—on all counts. If you have bought this book and after reading it think that your money was not well spent, contact me. I'll refund whatever you paid for it. That is for me a painless offer. No one could read this book and not think it was a marvelous bargain. Before even finishing it, most of us who read it will plan to read it more than once, probably many more times than once. I can guarantee that I will. I have about ten books in my library that I have read, reread, and will read again. They never fail to hit my heart and move me closer to God, sometimes when I feel very far away from him at the start. This book will raise the number of such books to eleven. Done deal.

The writing style of the book surprised me. Jeanie is an excellent writer and can write in different styles, but I expected this book to be simply a compilation of her blog articles about Wyndham's wisdom. Those articles were written for the most part like most books are, with sentence structure and length designed to flow in ways that make the reading easy and skimming possible. My expectations were in line for a bit of a shock.

Reading each of the brief chapters reminded me of reading the Book of Proverbs. Jeanie wrote in almost exactly that style. What is a proverb? Here are a few ideas: a short sentence that is full of meaning and sound advice; short sentences drawn from long experience; a brief popular epigram or maxim; a simple, concrete, traditional saying that expresses a perceived truth based on common sense or experience. My definition (probably original now, having forgotten the source): a short, pithy saying that is pregnant with meaning.

Chapter after chapter, this is the style. She writes short sentences, arranged in short paragraphs. This style just grabs you and captures your attention and makes its mark

Foreword

on your heart. While it was unexpected, especially since I am familiar with Jeanie's other writing, it was beyond refreshing. I couldn't skim through it, although I tried a couple of times. Each page seemed like another little treasure chest full of golden nuggets. I had to pause and think and pray. Of course, much is written in normal prose, but the overall impact to me was the proverbial style. Here are but a few examples from hundreds, and all of them will be made richer as you later read their contexts:

- Living a life for God begins from the inside out. It begins and ends with integrity.
- What a miry walk we walk when we let personalities rule our emotions, rather than principles of right and wrong.
- Creating a safe place comes from reassurance, a listening ear, the ability to relate, sharing how you understand or want to understand, vulnerability, and unconditional love.
- Wisdom understands that focusing (spiritually) on today is what prepares us for tomorrow. My faith must be strong today to prepare for the unknown tomorrow.
- Suffering empties us, carrying us to the broken place where God can fill us.
- "My occupation is dean of admissions at the University of Florida, but my *preoccupation* is the Kingdom of God." *(Jeanie's dad)*
- What often seemed urgent has since lost importance. What is truly important has become what is more urgent. *(In light of Wyndham's illness)*
- Too often, we view God as separated from us, the "audience," divided by the vast gulf of the orchestra pit. I picture my relationship with God as one in

which Jesus crossed the gulf of the pit and—extending his hand to me, in the audience—carried me to the stage of life to dance with him.

While I love the Book of Proverbs, it was written in another setting in a bygone age. Jeanie's book speaks to our modern setting. I suspect that if the Shaws lived in that bygone age, some of Wyndham's proverbial wisdom would have ended up in God's book, as well as that of Jeanie. Although the title of this book directs us toward Wyndham's wisdom, Jeanie wrote it all down in her words, complete with her own astute observations.

Jeanie's wisdom is intertwined with Wyndham's, as would be expected given their decades of being happily married and working together as a team of equals. Her wisdom grew exponentially as she faced the huge challenges of the past several years. In the wisdom arena, I think she and Wyndham are now pretty much on equal footing as she speaks in present tense and Wyndham speaks from eternity in past tense.

What I read compelled me to pause long enough to make phone calls and write letters (in the form of emails and phone texts) to connect with people. In short, my priorities got rearranged and corrected. It did move me to cry more than a few times, and not just because I know and love Wyndham and Jeanie deeply. Those little nuggets pierced my heart and made me ever so grateful for people in my life and thankful for life itself, all parts of it. They were reminders of God's principles and blessings that brought tears of repentance and tears of joy and gratitude.

Reading the book continued to soften my heart—over and over again. It stopped me in my tracks and moved me

Foreword

to do something with what I read, many times interrupting my reading as I got up and did it. A book that can do that for a person like me (who really needs it) is a book of inestimable value. Each brief chapter ends with a short paragraph calling us to reflect on what we have just read. This "For Reflection" part is followed by a brief written-out prayer. Somehow your heart enters that prayer and it ends up becoming your own. Such a helpful way to make the main point of the chapter find its way home to your soul!

And then we come to the final chapters, written by Wyndham's children and grandchildren while he was yet alive. Simply blow-away. I have no words. You will just have to read it for yourself. How could a man provide a foundation to build a family like his? OGK (only God knows). Prepare to stand in awe as you read the fine print of what produced the best results I've ever seen of following God's blueprint. In the words of Hebrews 11:4, Wyndham, though dead, still speaks. His family, yet alive, still speaks. I am excited with anticipation for you, the reader, as you begin what will be a life-altering experience. I need say no more. Just start reading.

INTRODUCTION

Every so often we meet individuals who have particularly meaningful and obvious gifts from God. Such was the case with Wyndham Shaw. When people encountered and interacted with him, his wisdom quickly became obvious. I believe God gave him a generous portion of wisdom, which has been often and well used to change many lives. His desire was always to please God, from the inside out.

I first met Wyndham at the University of Florida when he was a Resident Assistant on my then-boyfriend's dormitory floor. Even then, as a nineteen-year-old, I respected him as a man of wisdom and integrity. As he studied the Scriptures and learned more accurately and adequately how to follow them, he humbly responded and has been changing lives ever since.

The then-boyfriend and I felt bad for Wyndham on the weekends, as his then-girlfriend lived out of state, so we often invited him to join us on our Saturday night dates. The rest is history. We became best friends, fell in love, and were married in 1974. Forty-three ministry years, many houses, four children, eight grandchildren, countless adventures, and eight dogs later we have experienced life to the full, as promised by Jesus in John 10:10. There have been many dips and thrills on this roller coaster of life, but we have been richly blessed. I would heartily recommend this life and marriage to anyone, and we bow in gratitude to God for making it possible. Without his love and mercy, and his living and active words, we would not have had anything resembling this "life to the full."

For a long while, I have wanted to express some of the wisdom gleaned from Wyndham's life in writing so that as many as possible can gain from the life I observed, shared in, and loved for over four decades. I not only desired to honor him, but also to let this wisdom have farther-reaching effects. After seeking input from several friends, I decided to gather and share pieces of Wyndham's wisdom each Wednesday. This book is a collection of these writings, along with other chapters that have not yet been shared. My goal is to illustrate the ways godly wisdom can be applied to everyday living.

Wyndham's physical voice was soft and weak when I began writing, but his example remained loud and strong. Some of these chapters were written when he could still talk and move his hands. As my writings progressed, so did his disease. He suffered from a rare neurodegenerative disease called multiple system atrophy. It's a horrible disease we would wish on no one. Several years ago, my agile, athletic, active husband became wheelchair-bound, unable to carry out normal daily activities on his own. The disease continued to progress, eventually shutting down all bodily functions.

God still faithfully heard our many prayers, and we remained confident of several things: God loves us, he hears

Introduction

us, he is all-powerful, and he does not make mistakes. He will always give us exactly what we need. He is good all of the time. I am more convinced than ever that this world is not our home. Every day is a gift. Wyndham and I would begin our prayer together in the mornings with Lamentations 3:21–24:

> Yet this I call to mind
> and therefore I have hope:
>
> Because of the LORD's great love we are not
> consumed,
> for his compassions never fail.
> They are new every morning;
> great is your faithfulness.
> I say to myself, "The LORD is my portion;
> therefore I will wait for him."

Wyndham's prayers and resolve as he lived with this disease were to be grateful, courageous, faithful, and cheerful each day—which he did amazingly well. I told you he was a wise man. I made it my goal to have this same resolve.

The first piece of wisdom I will share exuded from his soul since his earliest days as a Christian. It comes from his all-time favorite Bible verse, 1 Timothy 1:5:

> The goal of this command is love, which comes
> from a pure heart and a good conscience and a
> sincere faith.

This is the wisdom he lived by. Living a life for God begins from the inside out. It begins and ends with integrity. Walking daily with sincerity of faith, purity of heart, and a clear conscience results in a life of love. Such is the wisdom I have watched him live...day after day.

As I share the wisdom I have learned through my relationship with Wyndham, I pray that you will gain more of God's wisdom and let that spread to all those around you. While this book is a collection of some of the nuggets of wisdom I published every Wednesday, more can be viewed on my website at jeaniesjourneys.com. Most of the chapters I have written, but some have been contributed by others who wished to share some wisdom they gained from Wyndham. The last section is a compilation of remembrances of his wisdom recounted by our family. I am deeply grateful for all the love, prayers, and support from our family and friends.

The chapters in this book, except for the last two, were written while Wyndham was still living and at different stages of his disease progression, and thus are written as such. They are not necessarily in chronological order. Each chapter ends with several thoughts for reflection along with a prayer, to help you better apply the wisdom illustrated to your own life.

May we all grow in the wisdom from above, thus more radiantly reflecting the glory of God in our lives.

1

WISDOM KNOWS
WHERE TO FIND WISDOM

Have you ever faced a situation in which you simply did not know what to do? I can think of many such times. I don't really enjoy those situations, as I prefer to have ready plans and solutions for problems. I enjoy the creativity in discovering plans of action, thinking perhaps if I brainstorm enough, ask enough questions, read enough books, use enough diagrams, or even "sleep on it," a great solution will emerge. While there are advantages to finding strategies and solving problems, there is also the accompanying temptation of self-reliance.

I can feel helpless when stuck without a plan of action, and so can be tempted to think that surely I can and should think of one. Therein lies the problem of self-reliance. I am challenged and inspired by the faithful and vulnerable attitude of Jehoshaphat in 2 Chronicles 20:12:

> Our God, will you not judge them? For we have no power to face this vast army that is attacking us. We do not know what to do, but our eyes are on you.

He stated for all to hear that he did not know what to do. Taking initiative, strategic thinking, and careful planning are good and helpful qualities, but these same qualities can also tempt us to forget how much we need God.

21

Instead of first inquiring of him, meditating on the Scriptures, and spending time in prayer, do we first let our minds race toward answers? When we don't know what to do, are we faithful enough to believe that God will bring answers, just as he did for Jehoshaphat?

Wisdom knows that wisdom comes from God:

> If any of you lacks wisdom, he should ask God, who gives generously to all without finding fault, and it will be given to him. (James 1:5)

Though Wyndham is gifted with wisdom, he continually seeks it from God. I have numerous mental images of him stopping to pray, fast, and inquire of God. Some of these times were while walking the power lines alone with God, many were with the family, some were before (and during) appointments and others were during conflicts or dilemmas. One time stands out to me during a season when our church went through a time of discipline and repentance. Troubled times. When he was faced with myriad difficult decisions, I saw Wyndham's attitude like that of Jehoshaphat in the scripture above. He did not know what to do, but his eyes focused on God.

Armed with his Bible and a songbook, he asked our son-in-law, who is also in the ministry, to accompany him to a cabin for a couple of days. For big strategy planning? An amazing think tank and discussion time? No. The time was devoted to singing, praying, and reading the Bible. Praising God. Enjoying friendship with God. Inquiring of God. That was it. That was his plan for gaining

Wisdom Knows Where to Find Wisdom

wisdom and strength (and peace) to go forward. I have often observed Wyndham going to God for wisdom, confident that he will give generously without finding fault.

Really, where else is there to go but to him? All roads to wisdom lead us to Jesus. Our best-laid plans are truly foolish if they are not born from God's wisdom. Wisdom knows where to find wisdom.

> Where is the wise person? Where is the teacher of the law? Where is the philosopher of this age? Has not God made foolish the wisdom of the world? For since in the wisdom of God the world through its wisdom did not know him, God was pleased through the foolishness of what was preached to save those who believe. Jews demand signs and Greeks look for wisdom, but we preach Christ crucified: a stumbling block to Jews and foolishness to Gentiles, but to those whom God has called, both Jews and Greeks, Christ the power of God and the wisdom of God. For the foolishness of God is wiser than human wisdom, and the weakness of God is stronger than human strength.
> (1 Corinthians 1:20–25)

FOR REFLECTION

Reflect on a time when you felt unsure how to handle a situation. What was your first response? Anxiety? Fear? Anger? Bingeing? Shutting down? Or did you find strength and wisdom in God *first*, going to him in prayer and seeking solace in his presence? If this is not your first response, how might you change that? Today, make it your first response to pray and read a scripture that speaks to your situation. Do this again tomorrow until it becomes your spiritual habit.

WEDNESDAYS WITH WYNDHAM

Father, many times I don't know what to do. In my self-reliance, I often try to figure things out on my own. In the busyness of the moment, I find it difficult to stop—to be still with you. I know you see all things and have all wisdom. Help me to first go to you in prayer and thanksgiving, asking you for wisdom and knowing you will answer. Help me listen to the guidance of your Spirit and to humbly hear your word. I give my angst, my decisions, my questions, and thoughts to you, Lord, thankful that you can carry them and provide the wisdom I need. In Jesus' name, Amen.

2

WISDOM KNOWS
YOU ARE STILL WHO YOU ARE

In the past, I've asked myself some seemingly strange questions. When I first contemplated my decision to follow Jesus, I asked myself, "Self, would you be willing to move to Africa if God asked you to? Would you stand up for Jesus if someone put a gun to your head and told you to disown him?" I don't know why I rehearsed these unlikely scenarios in my mind, as I now realize we more often are called to make less spectacular, daily decisions while following Jesus.

As crazy as it may seem, Wyndham and I *were* asked to move to Africa soon after arriving in Boston. We not only agreed to go, but had already begun preparing when the needs of the church there suddenly changed, and we were instead asked to stay in Boston. I never did have a gun put to my head, but I *did* have a knife put to my back as I then declared my devotion to Jesus. For real. But that's another story for another time. I have also asked myself, "Would you still have something to give if the things you valued most were taken?" This is a hard question, but my husband decisively answers this question with his life, as his health has been stripped away.

Though the wisdom I have already gained from Wyndham is invaluable, he still teaches me as I watch him

25

daily live out the answer to my question—"What would I still have, or who would I be, if things I value were taken away?"

Life has changed drastically over the last several years for Wyndham (and for me). He once loved to throw a football, hit a baseball, walk in the woods with his dog, and catch a big fish—or any fish. He loved to travel to help strengthen churches and loved to preach and teach. We felt useful as we counseled many couples on marriage and parenting. He led an amazing team of elders and was consulted on all kinds of difficult situations. Now he does none of those things. He can't throw a ball, stand, walk, fish, get in a boat, travel, preach, or teach. His energy only allows for minimal involvement in conversations that are "deep waters." He can't turn over in bed, transfer himself from his wheelchair to anywhere, get dressed, or sit without support. Fatigue is his constant companion, and his voice is often not strong enough to communicate clearly.

Too often we gain our confidence, satisfaction, and value according to what we can do. As we meet people, we

Wisdom Knows You are Still Who You Are

may be asked, "What do you do?" Depending on what we do, our answers may encourage or discourage us. We so easily place our identity and value in what we do that if (or more accurately when) things in our lives change, our contentment and joy come crashing down with the changes. In contrast, when our deepest foundation is built on Jesus and his words, we will never lose our confidence or contentment.

> "Therefore everyone who hears these words of mine and puts them into practice is like a wise man who built his house on the rock. The rain came down, the streams rose, and the winds blew and beat against that house; yet it did not fall, because it had its foundation on the rock."
> (Matthew 7:24–25)

Wyndham, as a wise man, built his foundation on the rock of Jesus and his words. Though the proverbial wind is howling and the streams are rising and beating against his body, nothing drowns the joy and confidence of who he is in Christ. No disease can take away his salvation or his purpose. Nothing can steal his joy, as he loves his family and is loved by them. No thing can keep him from caring and praying about those he loves.

Though he can no longer do the things he once did, his love for God and for people keeps him cheerful, courageous, grateful, and faithful. His knowledge of his salvation and of God's undying love for him keeps him hopeful. His focus on Jesus' example keeps him courageous. As often as we pray and bask in the love we share for each other and our family, his eyes always fill with tears of indescribable gratitude for what God has done for him and for us.

No situation in life can change who we are in Christ or take away the gifts God has lavished on us—unless we let them. Wisdom knows that when we can no longer do what we once did, we remain who we are in Christ. Nothing and no one can take this away from us.

> Who shall separate us from the love of Christ? Shall trouble or hardship or persecution or famine or nakedness or danger or sword? As it is written:
>
> "For your sake we face death all day long;
>   we are considered as sheep to be slaughtered."
>
> No, in all these things we are more than conquerors through him who loved us.
>
> For I am convinced that neither death nor life, neither angels nor demons, neither the present nor the future, nor any powers, neither height nor depth, nor anything else in all creation, will be able to separate us from the love of God that is in Christ Jesus our Lord. (Romans 8:35–39)

For Reflection

Consider where you find your value and identity. Are you more eager to share with others about your job, your talents, and your education, or about your relationship with God? If you lost your job, your health, or even a loved one, would you still believe you are loved, have purpose, and have something of great value to offer? If not, write down and reflect on scriptures that can remind you of your identity and purpose in Christ.

Father, the world around me tempts me to put my value on worldly things. Even if everything I value in this world were stripped from me, may I find my strength, value, and purpose in you alone. As I live today, help me to live with eternity in mind. As I look in the mirror, help me focus my identity on who you say that I am. From this strength, let me give to those around me, no matter my circumstance. Fill me with confidence that nothing can take your love from me. Thank you for showing me what is truly important in life, and help me keep my eyes focused on these things. In Jesus' name, Amen.

3

WISDOM
Always Leads by Example

When Wyndham and I were dating I was very "artsy and craftsy." Decoupage was a popular craft, and one day I presented Wyndham with a decoupaged plaque that read:

> The world has yet to see what God will do with and through and for and by the man who is fully and totally consecrated to him. I will strive my utmost to be that man.

It was nothing beautiful to look at, but Wyndham treasured the plaque because of the message. He has referred to that plaque many times throughout his life—as he has lived that message and striven to be that man. He strove for this, not because he wanted to be a leader, but because he desired to please God. He delighted in God. He longed to fulfill God's purpose for his life—fully confident that God had a true intention for his life. He strove to continue to grow and to dedicate his life to this higher purpose (thus, consecrating himself). Because of this, his life has impacted countless people for God.

Wisdom Always Leads by Example

It would be easy, now that he is ill and can't do much, to think about himself and his difficult situation. After all, he spent most of his life serving God. He could easily rationalize: *It's time to think about me and my misfortune. I've served a long time and am tired and ill. Let my past be enough.*

However, throughout the days God gives him, I still see Wyndham fully and wholly consecrating himself to God—praying that the Father will continue to work with and through and for and by him.

When things are hard or when we are older or when we have been a disciple of Jesus for a long time, it can be easy to think we've served long enough and have stored up enough "good deeds" to last for a lifetime; however, wisdom knows you never quit leading by example. In attitude. In purpose. In kindness. In love. In contentment. In gratitude. In courage. In integrity. In compassion. All of these qualities impact others, perhaps even more than our deeds.

Jesus never quit. On the cross, he forgave. On the cross, he thought of his mother and of his dear friend John. On the cross, he thought of you and me and the satisfaction our changed lives would bring his anguished soul:

> When he sees all that is accomplished by his
>   anguish,
>   he will be satisfied.
> And because of his experience,
>   my righteous servant will make it possible
> for many to be counted righteous,
>   for he will bear all their sins.
> (Isaiah 53:11 NLT)

After Jesus was resurrected, he cooked breakfast for his disciples. He walked and talked with them. He loved them.

He believed in them and entrusted everything to them. His last action as he ascended was to bless them:

> When he had led them out to the vicinity of Bethany, he lifted up his hands and blessed them. While he was blessing them, he left them and was taken up into heaven (Luke 24:50–51).

Jesus never quit leading by his example—thinking of others all the way to heaven. Wisdom knows that we never outgrow leading by example.

FOR REFLECTION

Ask yourself: *Do I desire to be a person who is wholly consecrated to God, thus allowing my life to impact others around me? If I don't have such a desire, why might this be? What does my current example show about who or what is most important to me?* Share with another disciple one decision that will help you become more fully consecrated to God so that they can pray for you and help you in this endeavor.

> *Father, I get tempted to think of my desires, no longer desiring to give and serve. Thank you that you never quit giving. Jesus, I know you often retreated to spend time with the Father, and I need the same. Please, fill me with your Spirit so that I don't run out of joy. Fill me with your peace, patience, and wisdom so that I can give out of the excess of what you have given to me. Help me desire total consecration to you, becoming more like you every day. Father, the world has yet to see the one who is fully and wholly consecrated to you. Help me both to desire and to become that person. In Jesus' name, Amen.*

4

WISDOM KNOWS
"TENTATIVE"

Have you ever boldly espoused your opinion, only to realize that you were totally wrong? Or do you know someone who espouses opinions forcefully and often? Wyndham has a phrase for this practice: "Often wrong, but never in doubt!" I find this scenario happens most frequently in matters of opinion and memory and results in statements such as:

- I absolutely know I left this on your desk.
- We turn right here. I'm sure.
- I have looked there. It's not there.
- You just need to let your child cry. They will definitely go to sleep.
- You shouldn't let them cry. They won't go to sleep.
- If you take this supplement, it will cure you. It does this and this and this...
- If you eat this, it will kill you.

You may have heard (or said) all of the above, spoken with absolute surety.

There's a scripture for this practice:

Fools find no pleasure in understanding
but delight in airing their own opinions.
(Proverbs 18:2)

33

In contrast, a wise person seeks to understand, and is prudent in airing their opinions. Sure, there are things to which we should hold with absolute conviction. Truths about God and his word are at the top of this list. For these, we must be bold and unapologetic, even when these truths are in opposition to the culture of our world—which they are.

However, in opinions (and even our memories, which we often view as factual), Wyndham has taught me the value of speaking tentatively. And in order to be tentative, we must be calm. We must seek understanding. We must be humble to be tentative. And we must be eager to keep peace in our relationships in order to be tentative. Yet we (I) can easily get "riled up," sure of what we (I) think, and sure that our (my) memory is rock-solid correct.

I think of this word "tentative" often in my conversations. This nugget of wisdom has served me well. Wyndham and I have striven to implement it in our conversations for years. To accomplish this, we decided many years ago to exercise a habit that reminds us that we are not always right. When we discover we are wrong in something we have confidently stated, we say (yes, out loud) to each other, "I was wrong, and you were right." It's been a good practice.

Let me define tentativeness by rewording the above statements:

- *I absolutely know I left this on your desk.*
  With tentativeness, this can be reworded as: *I may not remember it accurately, but I seem to recall leaving this on your desk.*
- *We turn right here. I'm sure.*
  Tentative: *I think we turn right here.*

Wisdom Knows "Tentative"

- *I have looked there. It's not there.*
  Tentative: *I looked there once, but didn't find it. I can try again.*
- *You just need to let your child cry. They will definitely go to sleep.*
  Tentative: *I've found at times it has worked for me to let my baby "cry it out" to go to sleep.*
- *You shouldn't let them cry. They won't go to sleep.*
  Tentative: *You may find this to work or not, but for me, my baby got more worked up the longer he/she cried. This is what helped me...*
- *If you take this supplement, it will cure you. It does this and this and this...*
  Tentative: *I'm sure you have heard many opinions, but this supplement has helped me, and I'm excited about it. Let me know if you want to know more.*
- *If you eat this, it will kill you.*
  Tentative: *I don't want to intrude, but I read some research that troubled me. I made this choice because of these reasons. I won't be pushy, but I can send you some information if you would like it.*

Without tentativeness, Wyndham's wise phrase too often applies: "Often wrong, but never in doubt." The Scriptures teach in James 4:6b, "God opposes the proud but gives grace to the humble" (NLT).

The truth is, people also oppose the proud but give grace to the humble. May we never doubt what is truth, but speak (with tentativeness) to gain wisdom and understanding in matters not pertaining to salvation.

For Reflection

Think about your last disagreement or argument with someone, particularly a family member. As you think over the godly qualities of gentleness and humility, how did you do? Today, practice speaking tentatively. It may be difficult at first. You may find it helpful to let those with whom you most interact know that you are working on speaking tentatively. This takes humility, but that's the goal, right?

> *Father, you call me to be humble, to be gentle, to be quick to listen and slow to speak. These are easier to read than to do. Lord, help me take my thoughts and words captive. By your grace and mercy, you have treated me with complete love that I don't deserve. Please help me as I strive to be tentative when I speak my opinions and feelings, and help me be aware of what I say and how I say it. Help me not to blame or shame others. Help me to see the best in them. Father, please help me be bold and courageous concerning your words and your teachings. In all situations, help me speak with love and humility. Thank you, Father, for hearing my prayer.*

5

WISDOM DIGS
IN THE RIGHT PLACES

The purposes of a person's heart are deep waters,
but one who has insight draws them out.
(Proverbs 20:5)

Many times, I don't immediately know what I'm feeling, and Wyndham has often not only helped to draw out my emotions (especially when the feelings weren't between us) but also helped me understand their source. Once I understand the source of my emotions, it's much easier to accurately adjust my perception.

The following descriptions of wisdom involve digging. The first is from Kitty Chiles and the second from Gordon Ferguson.

Bud and Kitty Chiles became dear friends when we worked together for HOPE worldwide. Wyndham and I were novices in the nonprofit humanitarian world and learned much from their vast experience. Kitty shares the impact that Wyndham's "digging below the surface" had on her life. In the entry that follows hers, our dear friend Gordon also explains the wisdom in "excavating beneath the surface."

FROM KITTY:
I am grateful for this opportunity to express my love and respect for Wyndham, a spiritual giant in my

37

life. While our years working with him and Jeanie were too brief, they made a profound impact on me. I will share one short interaction that I have carried in my heart for close to fifteen years.

On one occasion, Bud, Wyndham, Jeanie, and I were talking about several challenging relationships. I, especially, was struggling with having the courage (and love) to deal with a conflict and work through it. At one point, Wyndham looked at me and told me I was perhaps the most easily accused person he has ever known. I was stunned. No one had ever described me as "accused" in my then twenty years as a Christian. He went on to tell me ways this perception was playing out in my life and was crippling me spiritually; how Satan (the great accuser) was using it in my life. My personal antennae were so far extended that I was perceiving things about myself that were untrue. It was affecting my relationships across the board.

Since that day, I have been increasingly aware of this spiritual and emotional handicap, yet Wyndham's words have continually encouraged me. I have developed an awareness of Satan's schemes in my life and how I can overcome them with God's word and the wisdom of godly relationships like the one with Wyndham, whose wisdom and perception have changed my life. And I know that this godly quality

Wisdom Digs in the Right Places

has enriched the lives of all those that he has touched with it. Thank you, brother.

FROM GORDON:

When we moved to Boston a couple of days before the dawn of 1988, Wyndham and Jeanie picked us up at the airport. (We were paired as discipleship partners.) They had no clue what this relationship was going to mean to their life and schedule, trust me! I was a mess when we moved. If you are interested in seeing more of these details, read Chapter 9 in my book, *Fairy Tales Do Come True*. My being a mess led to our marriage being about the same. The Shaws started on a path that took us all through repeated marriage counseling sessions.

To my knowledge, they were the first to employ what we later were to call "marriage reconstructions." Wyndham is nothing if not thorough, and thankfully, along with it, patient. He left no stone unturned as he dug into our relationship, going all the way back to when we were dating twenty-five-plus years prior.

At times, I remember being somewhat incredulous at the little details Theresa recalled—details about how I had hurt her. When I got ticked off and was being prideful and saying stupid things, Wyndham

would say something like, "Bro, just be quiet and let her share what's on her heart." He was determined to dig out anything from the past that might be impeding the present. Let me just say that it was an arduous process—but a process that changed my life and our marriage!

My good brother's wisdom in this situation often went against the grain of conventional wisdom. That quality showed up many times during the years that we worked together in Boston, but I saw it early on and close up during that marriage counseling process. Conventional wisdom (much more conventional than wise) was that husbands were to blame for all marriage problems. After all, they were the leaders, right? And if leaders, responsible for all failures!

Wyndham flatly rejected that viewpoint, although it was definitely the prevailing one in the church in the late 1980s. I think it would have been obvious to almost any sensible person that I was the main problem in our marriage. Thus, it would have been understandable if I was the only focus in his counseling. However, while I was Wyndham's main target, he didn't let my little wife's cuteness and submissiveness throw him off track. He dealt with her stuff too—very patiently and gently, but thoroughly.

Her view of authority figures had been seriously damaged by many in her experience, me being one on that sad list. Wyndham won her heart over for life, becoming in the process the most trusted male in her world. He also became one of my most trusted, a man of wisdom who will be tightly bound in Theresa's and my hearts forever!

Wisdom is not afraid to lovingly dig...and cares enough to do so.

Wisdom Digs in the Right Places

FOR REFLECTION

Ask yourself: *Are there areas in my life where I feel stuck? If so, do I willingly seek trusted and godly counsel to help me dig through the obstacles, in order to help me discover any sins or hurts that I may have stuffed for many years and which have held me back?* If not, make the call, talk to a friend, or do whatever it takes to get help getting "unstuck." If you see someone stuck or unaware, do you lovingly pray for and with them, encouraging them as you speak the Scriptures in love to them? Determine whether this is a practice you are serious about, and if not, take action this week to set this kind of honest, loving discipleship in motion.

Father, thank you for digging deeply into my life to find me and to show me my sin and my need for you. Please show me, Father, areas where I am stuck and need further understanding and growth. Help me not to be afraid to dig deeper, knowing that there is no fear in love and perfect love casts out fear. Give me the wisdom to know when to lovingly and patiently dig deeper into my own life and with those whom I love in order to bring us all closer to you. Search me Lord, and know my heart. Thank you for nurturing and growing me, even though it doesn't always feel good. I love you, Lord. In Jesus' name, Amen.

6

WISDOM IS
A UTILITY PLAYER

I enjoy baseball and am unashamedly a Red Sox fan. If you're not so inclined, stay with me here, as the Red Sox actually have nothing to do with this section. In baseball, I know the names of many pitchers and homerun hitters, but I know the names of few to no utility players. Utility players are team members who play various positions as they are needed. Most often, these players aren't household names, but their contributions are crucial to their teams. Utility players must be flexible, capable, and not too attached to their favorite positions.

The Scriptures speak of "utility players" who were chosen as such because they were full of the Spirit and wisdom. Do you quickly recognize the names of Nicanor, Timon, Procorus, Nicolas, and Parmenas? Probably not.

Stephen and Philip are better known…but these other guys were also full of wisdom and the Spirit. Who were these people? Luke tells us about these men:

> In those days when the number of disciples was increasing, the Hellenistic Jews among them complained against the Hebraic Jews because their widows were being overlooked in the daily distribution of food. So the Twelve gathered all the disciples together and said, "It would not be right for us to

Wisdom is a Utility Player

neglect the ministry of the word of God in order to wait on tables. Brothers and sisters, choose seven men from among you who are known to be full of the Spirit and wisdom. We will turn this responsibility over to them and will give our attention to prayer and the ministry of the word."

This proposal pleased the whole group. They chose Stephen, a man full of faith and of the Holy Spirit; also Philip, Procorus, Nicanor, Timon, Parmenas, and Nicolas from Antioch, a convert to Judaism. They presented these men to the apostles, who prayed and laid their hands on them.

So the word of God spread. The number of disciples in Jerusalem increased rapidly, and a large number of priests became obedient to the faith.
(Acts 6:1–7)

These men were chosen because they were spiritual and wise. What was their first great and noble assignment born from their wisdom and spirituality?

Distribution of food to the Grecian widows. "Why?" you might ask.

Because it was needed.

Wyndham has switched roles numerous times throughout his work in the ministry. Some roles have been high profile, and some have not. He has embraced each one equally, as his desire has always been to be used by God wherever he was most needed...as a player, a coach, or player-coach. (FYI, he's the cute one pictured on the back row, second little ballplayer

from the left.) He was not overly attached to a certain role, though certainly some he enjoyed more than others. He did not allow himself to be distracted from his purpose when changes happened.

I more often find change difficult and am more at ease sticking with what I am most confident and comfortable doing, and also what I enjoy the most. At times I've changed roles "kicking and screaming" inside while complying outwardly. Even now, I have been given a different work role, and Wyndham's wisdom tumbles through my heart…because this change is not what I want to do. Wisdom calls me to be a utility player. What does it call you to be?

God always brings blessings when I respond with humility. It does not always bring immediate joy; however, there is always joy, peace, and victory in godly surrender.

I am so grateful for Wyndham's willingness to be a utility player, for whatever the need at hand. True wisdom is born from this kind of humility. As the Acts 6 utility players joyfully  fulfilled their roles, God's word spread and many became disciples. You may not remember their names, but God does, and he used their willing service to build a mighty team.

For Reflection

Transitions are often hard. They test our faith and trust in God. As you have encountered transitions in your life, especially ones you did not choose, reflect on how you felt

Wisdom is a Utility Player

when they happened. What helped you finally gain peace in these transitions? Reflect on ways you think you could more faithfully handle transitions, and decide how you can continue to serve God and others despite current or future changes in your life situation.

Jesus, I know that no one experienced transition such as you did, going from union with God in heaven to birth in a barn and death on a cross. Father, you emptied yourself through Jesus as he showed us what it means to love. As I think of ways I respond or am responding to transition, help me to have the attitude of emptying myself. I cannot do this without trusting you, and I praise you that you are completely trustworthy. Father, in whatever ways you want to use me, please do so. This is scary to pray, but I can say it because I know and rely on the love you have for me. You are love. Help me to handle transitions with trust in you, and like Jesus, help me say, "Your will be done." I trust you my Abba, my Father.

7

WISDOM SPEAKS APTLY

It happened to me yesterday and again today. In fact, few days go by without someone telling me something like this:

> Wyndham believed in me, and his words gave me the vision to see myself as God sees me, not how I see myself. When I didn't believe in myself, his directed and encouraging words (full of vision for me) changed my life.

They tell me what he said, when he said it, and how the words affected their lives. Wisdom knows the power of words aptly spoken.

A word aptly spoken
    is like apples of gold in settings of silver.
Like an earring of gold or an ornament
      of fine gold is
    a wise man's rebuke to a listening ear.
Like the coolness of snow at harvest time
    is a trustworthy messenger to those who
      send him;
    he refreshes the spirit of his masters.
(Proverbs 25:11–13 NIV 1984)

While most of us can remember words that damaged, fortunately, we can also remember specific words that gave us the courage to keep going and the faith to believe what

Wisdom Speaks Aptly

we couldn't see. Words that reminded us of our value to God and to others.

I watched and learned as I heard Wyndham continually look into people's eyes and offer them vision and hope for their lives. He told them ways God could use them to make a difference in this world—and that they are needed. I heard him give loving correction when needed, yet those words also ended with vision and hope.

I get too busy and must remind myself to have these conversations. I have good intentions and think these things about others, but thinking them and taking the time to express them are two different things. Truth is, these conversations take consideration and deliberateness. After a while, they will more naturally flow from our mouths. When I take the time to think through who, when, and how to encourage, it really does make a difference. I am motivated toward love and good deeds when I'm encouraged.

> Let us hold unswervingly to the hope we profess, for he who promised is faithful. And let us consider how we may spur one another on toward love and good deeds, not giving up meeting together, as some are in the habit of doing, but encouraging one another—and all the more as you see the Day approaching. (Hebrews 10:23–25)

This scripture tells me I need to do this more and more! There is more that's needed than just "showing up" to church (though that's a great start, as we surely can't have these conversations without being with each other). God wants us to encourage each other while meeting together.

So, beginning today, please join me in being deliberate

with someone—taking time to encourage them in a specific and meaningful way. Not only will you be wiser, but words aptly spoken can change a life for the better.

FOR REFLECTION

Consider a time you were encouraged by someone's words to you; words that called you higher spiritually and helped you believe that God values you and has a purpose for your life. Reflect on what they said and how they said it. Take a few moments before the next time the church meets together to consider two individuals you can encourage. Are you willing to take the time needed to grow in your ability to speak "apt" words?

> *Perfect Father, thank you for your words that both pierce and comfort. Your words give me life, hope, and purpose. Your words show me your strength and your tender concern. Please help me to consider my words, and to speak words that encourage and build faith. Help me to take initiative in conversations for the purpose of encouraging and building up. Give me insight into ways that I can touch those who need a word of encouragement and strength, and to notice the expressions and body language of those who are discouraged. Please help me to be more concerned with what others need than how I feel. I depend on you. In Jesus' name, Amen.*

8

WISDOM FINDS
THE HIGH ROAD

It was a pivotal time in my life. A time when I could have sold my soul to bitterness. Thankfully, Wyndham's wisdom (and humility) prevailed.

We had been in the ministry for eight years. I was twenty-eight years old and Wyndham was thirty. He had been preaching in a traditional type church for three years. We had led campus ministry for the previous five years, but this was his first preaching job. The church was growing, but the leadership was not united. In fact, one of the leaders would stand at the back door after Wyndham came down from the pulpit and pass out negative literature about us to the people who were leaving.

One woman called and swore at me, and I never even knew why. We were away one week when one of the leaders called and told my husband he should find a new job, as he wouldn't be able to stay there. Fired. The reason stated was this: "We don't have any problem with what you are preaching. It's all in the Bible. The problem some people are having is that when you come out of the pulpit, you expect people to follow it! And they don't want to change."

I was angry with the leaders and their decisions. I felt we had been wronged and were treated unfairly. That was true. I felt, as James and John (in their immaturity) stated

49

in Luke 9:54, like calling down fire from heaven to destroy them.

As Wyndham delivered his last sermon, I waited for him to "let them have it"—firmly rebuking them. Instead, he took the high road. He called them to follow Jesus but then apologized for anything he had ever done to hurt anyone.

What?! I then struggled with my husband. Why didn't he let them have it! After all, this was their problem. Bitterness was growing in my heart, but Wyndham understood the wisdom that comes from God.

> Who is wise and understanding among you? Let them show it by their good life, by deeds done in the humility that comes from wisdom. But if you harbor bitter envy and selfish ambition in your hearts, do not boast about it or deny the truth. Such "wisdom" does not come down from heaven but is earthly, unspiritual, demonic. For where you have envy and selfish ambition, there you find disorder and every evil practice.
>
> But the wisdom that comes from heaven is first of all pure; then peace-loving, considerate, submissive, full of mercy and good fruit, impartial and sincere. Peacemakers who sow in peace reap a harvest of righteousness. (James 3:13–18)

He found the high road and took it, never giving in to bitterness, but trusting that God would take care of us. We had two young children, I was pregnant, and we had nowhere to go. We simply needed to be humble and to trust God. I did need to have some talks with the elders and also some soul-searching times with God, which I did.

I realized that Jesus could have given in to sin even as he hung on the cross. Perhaps he faced his greatest temp-

Wisdom Finds the High Road

tation while on the cross: the temptation to be bitter. He was unimaginably mistreated, yet he said of the angry crowd as they spat and swore and crucified him, "Father, forgive them, for they do not know what they are doing" (Luke 23:34). As I read this, I thought, *What do you mean? Of course, they knew! Why did he say that?*

I do believe they still needed to repent and be baptized to be forgiven (Acts 2:36–38). But perhaps Jesus said these words to rid his own heart of any temptation toward bitterness. Since Jesus was not bitter, what right did I have to be bitter? I don't deserve forgiveness, but Jesus gave it to me.

So I let it go, and following the example of Wyndham's "wisdom from above," truly forgave. God's word was still true, and his plan for the church was still his only plan. I have hurt others too, so who am I to hold on to hurt? I shudder to think where this bitterness would have led me had my husband not taken the high road. I could have lost my soul had I held on.

Soon after this happened, a brother who had been converted in our campus ministry asked if we would be willing to move where he lived to start a church. Thirteen disciples were there and were willing to support us. One of the families invited us (along with our two girls and a child on the way) to live with them. We had no insurance and no money—but a lot of faith. God blessed that decision and never deserted us. Instead, he blessed us.

We all have temptations to grow bitter. Yet we all can make the decision to take the high road. Which road will you travel? Wisdom finds the high road.

For Reflection

What comes to your mind as the most hurtful thing you have experienced, both in the past and recently? As you reflect on the way Jesus forgave those who put him on the cross, do you believe you can also forgive those who have hurt you? Consider times when you did not take the high road when you were hurt. What did that look like and what did it accomplish? Pray through your hurts and ask God to help you take the high road. Do you need to have any conversations? If you are unsure how to take the high road, pray, read the Bible, and ask a trusted and mature Christian to show you what that road would look like.

Father, I confess that at times it is hard to forgive. I depend on your Spirit in order to do this. I cannot do it on my own. Jesus, I am in awe of the way you were misunderstood, scourged, beaten, spat upon, and crucified and yet you said, "Father forgive them..." Help me, Father, to entrust myself to you who judges justly, and to forgive as I have been forgiven. Search my heart and rid me of any bitterness. Where I need to have conversations, give me a spirit of love and forgiveness. Please, Father, help me be both honest and humble. Increase my faith, Father, so I might forgive seventy times seven. I commit this to you, knowing that you are a forgiving God.

9

WISDOM KNOWS
LOVE INVOLVES ACTION

by Gordon Ferguson

Jesus asked many questions, questions that need answers. In John 21:17, Jesus asks a poignant question of Peter:

> The third time he said to him, "Simon son of John, do you love me?"
> Peter was hurt because Jesus asked him the third time, "Do you love me?" He said, "Lord, you know all things; you know that I love you."
> Jesus said, "Feed my sheep."

The biblical context shows that Peter was smitten by the question. There are perhaps some subtleties involved in the Greek language here, but the question, "Do you love me?" is no doubt a probing one. Jesus taught that love for God must involve heart, soul, mind, and strength (Mark 12:30). Considering these, do I really love him? Do you? A probing question indeed!

I was raised in a legalistic religious setting and rebelled against it. Both the setting and my rebellion produced a lot of guilt inside me that has been difficult to get rid of. It is easy for me to question my love for God, and honestly, his love for me. At best, I'm an imperfect being, try as I might.

I am one of the members of what might be described as the "accused conscience" crowd. Therefore, it is easy to wonder whether I've done enough or been good enough to say with all honesty that I really love God.

I think back to a conversation with Wyndham that led to a pearl of wisdom that has helped me with my guilty-conscience struggles. We were discussing a leader whom we both knew, although Wyndham knew him far better than I did. The person had experienced some serious marriage problems, and at the end of that painful trial, had decided to leave God. As we discussed his plight and his actions, Wyndham said something like this: "You know, I think maybe the best way to show God that we love him is to hang in no matter what we are going through."

As I thought about it, I had one of those "Aha!" moments. Agape love is not just a feeling and perhaps not even primarily a feeling—it must include actions, especially when those actions are hard to muster. What loving parent ever wanted to get up in the middle of the night to clean the floor after a sick child emptied their stomach on it? Similar examples could be multiplied.

Here is where the definition of a true friend comes in. "A friend loves at all times, and a brother is born for a time of adversity" (Proverbs 17:17). When I think about who my real friends are, I think about those who have seen the worst of me and still stay with me. Wyndham has seen me at my best and at my worst, and his friendship remains constant.

His practical explanation of what love for God really means has been demonstrated in his love for me. If there is a friend who sticks closer than a brother (Proverbs 18:24), Wyndham is that friend. Using him as a human

Wisdom Knows Love Involves Action

starting point, it shouldn't be difficult to imagine God doing at least as well as he does! Of course, God is infinitely better at loving than even Wyndham, but Wyndham being able to love me at my worst helps me to understand and accept God's love—even at my worst.

God's word comes in at least two forms: the written form and the human example of what is written. Jesus was the ultimate human example of God's heart; those like  Jesus are real-life examples in the present tense. Okay, Lord, I may not feel all that I ought to feel, but I confessed Jesus as Lord, and I will never back down! Do I love you? Imperfectly, but yes. Thank you, Wyndham!

FOR REFLECTION

Ask yourself: *Do I often feel like I can't do enough to earn Jesus' love? Do I sometimes question God's love for me?* Remember that you haven't quit! You are reading this and reflecting on ways to grow. Write a short letter of what you think God might say to you as you keep on striving to follow him. Then, reply to that letter, committing to God that you will never quit.

> *Loving Father, I confess that at times I question your love for me. Forgive me. You have held nothing back to show your love, and for this, I praise you and honor you. Help me feel your for me love and believe what you say about it. Thank you that you will never leave me. Father, I commit that no matter what, I won't quit. Help*

WEDNESDAYS WITH WYNDHAM

me to know that you don't require perfection, only my whole heart. It is yours, Father. Through Jesus, I pray this prayer. Amen.

10

WISDOM IS IMPARTIAL

But the wisdom that comes from heaven is first of all
pure; then peace-loving, considerate, submissive,
full of mercy and good fruit, *impartial* and sincere.
(James 3:17, emphasis added)

Impartial is hard. Especially when it concerns people
with whom we are partial (duh)—our family and friends.
When friends and family are involved, it's easy to be ruled
by emotions rather than reality.

How different would your decisions, your counsel, your
reactions, and your opinions be if "nameless individuals"
were part of the situations you evaluated or conflicts you
sought to resolve?

Wyndham has often been considered "a safe place," in
part because of his wisdom to be impartial. One's position
or relationship to him really doesn't matter. This did not
always come easily, however. He learned wisdom from
God as he sought to determine what was right, not who
was right. What a miry walk we walk when we let personalities rule our emotions, rather than principles of right and
wrong.

Principle over personality.

Wyndham practices and teaches an axiom: *What's the
biblical principle? What is right?*

Jesus, in Mark 12:14, is seen among men as a man of integrity:

> They came to him and said, "Teacher, we know you are a man of integrity. You aren't swayed by others, because you pay no attention to who they are; but you teach the way of God in accordance with the truth. Is it right to pay taxes to Caesar or not?"

How I admire this quality in Jesus. How hard this quality has been for me, one who has often been a people pleaser, wanting everyone happy. I have worked hard to overcome this. Could the description of Jesus be said of us? Or would it more likely read: *You are often swayed by personalities because you pay attention to who they are and how they respond, stretching God's truth in accordance with your emotions.* Ouch.

I must often ask who I am most trying to please—God, or someone else. God, or me. (I can be partial to myself as well.)

I've often watched Wyndham imitate this quality of Jesus as he made hard decisions, unpopular decisions, "reacted to" decisions—all while seeking to be impartial and to practice principle over personality. But like I said earlier, this quality has also made him sought-after as a "safe place."

How does partiality/impartiality play out in our lives?

- When we are close to a husband or a wife in a marriage and take sides without hearing both versions of the matter, and subsequently fail to point both

Wisdom is Impartial

back to the Scriptures
- When our child appears to be wronged by someone and our hair bristles, but we don't hear the "other side of the story"
- When someone we know is hurt by someone whom they see as an authority figure, and we protect either the authority figure or the other person without hearing both out. (Proverbs 18:17 is such an important teaching of wisdom: "The first to speak seems right, until someone comes forward and cross-examines.")
- When we assume someone is "more right" because of their education, standing in society, or even ethnicity
- When we are asked to do something shady by a superior and we give in, knowing if we don't do it our job could be in jeopardy
- When we listen to and participate in put-downs or gossip, assuming the information is accurate and needs to be spread
- When we realize that someone we love is not following the Scriptures, but they are really nice and sincere, so we just let it slide so as not to create any discomfort

Do we value what is right over who is right? Do we choose principle over personality? Which ones win in our lives? Wisdom from above is impartial. Principle over personality, and holding to what is right over who is right is not "loveless," but expresses sincere love for another.

Impartiality exhibits true, unconditional love. Partiality is sentimental, but not loving. Partiality creates false security and leaves others with greater concern over what we think than what God says. That's not real love. Jesus spoke the way of God in accordance with the truth while embodying perfect love and extreme grace.

Partiality is subjective, rather than objective. This creates insecurity because it's based on feelings rather than a truth that does not change. Therefore, partiality is inconsistent. Impartiality brings security, maybe not always felt in the short run, but true over the long haul. We all need advocates in our lives, but we need advocacy backed with truth.

I can often want someone to take my side, but I do not want this at the expense of truth. While I always know I'm deeply loved by my husband, I also count on his impartial counsel and am eternally grateful for it. I'm thankful that as an elder he takes seriously this charge:

> I charge you, in the sight of God and Christ Jesus and the elect angels, to keep these instructions without partiality, and to do nothing out of favoritism. (1 Timothy 5:21)

FOR REFLECTION

Consider the questions above to help you determine how impartial you are. What is more important to you as shown by your actions: What is right? Or who is right? The principle of a situation? Or the personality that is at the forefront of the issue? Consider the consequences when choosing the latter. Determine to ask these questions whenever you encounter situations that tempt you to be partial.

Almighty Father, thank you that you are truth, but at the same time, you are full of grace. Please guide me as I strive to love the truth, and rid my life of partiality that

Wisdom is Impartial

keeps me from believing or expressing the truth. I am comforted by knowing that you are an impartial, loving, and merciful God. Please help me have such confidence in you and your word that truth is my friend. Empower me to be more like Jesus, who was full of grace and truth. As I pray, I am humbled by your perfection and my imperfection. I rely on your grace and your love. Thank you, Father.

11

WISDOM BREAKS BARRIERS

by Sam Powell

I appreciate Sam's words on barriers that exist and need to be broken. As I read his thoughts, I considered barriers in my life. Today, on the way to a meeting, a huge truck was stuck on the sloping pavement of a driveway, blocking the road in front of me. I had two choices. Give up and go home, or find a way past the barrier. Breaking through the barrier involved driving through a portion of someone's front yard (no damage was done), and it also involved some forms of courage and decisiveness. "What will the people in the car behind me think? What if I can't clear the barrier and I get stuck?"

Barriers of many kinds appear often and most anywhere. Do you get stuck, and turn around and go back home thinking, "Oh well, I tried," or do you push through? Breaking barriers requires wisdom in order to determine what needs to be done, followed by courage and decisiveness to follow through.

Jesus broke through all kinds of barriers for us (most importantly, the one separating us from God) and showed us the heart we need to break through barriers.

So in Christ Jesus you are all children of God
through faith, for all of you who were baptized into

Wisdom Breaks Barriers

Christ have clothed yourselves with Christ. There is neither Jew nor Gentile, neither slave nor free, nor is there male and female, for you are all one in Christ Jesus. If you belong to Christ, then you are Abraham's seed, and heirs according to the promise. (Galatians 3:26–29)

FROM SAM:

Breaking the Spiritual Barrier

I met Wyndham in the Spring of 1975. I was a freshman at North Carolina State University, and he was the campus minister. God indeed does move in mysterious ways his wonders to perform. I think about the barriers where the Lord used Wyndham to break into my life.

Wyndham discussed the costs of becoming a disciple of Jesus with me. My life had been about women, partying, and all the wrong things. I never thought I could or would be a Christian. The spiritual barrier for me was not only overcoming my sinful life but also believing and understanding that being a Christian meant being a man of strength, integrity, conviction, and character. Wyndham broke the barrier of how I viewed men who followed Jesus. He most definitely broke down the barrier of how I viewed ministers. It wasn't just the absence of robes and collars, but he was a man of deep conviction and intensity for God. He also liked sports and could talk about them in a practical and knowledgeable way. This was a far cry from television evangelists I saw and from those in the churches familiar to me.

Breaking the Racial Barrier

When I initially visited the Brooks Avenue church in the mid '70s I thought it would be my first and last visit there. There was just a handful of black people in the church and one black guy in the campus ministry, to whom I could not relate. Wyndham, the young campus minister, and many others showed me the love of God that could break down racial walls. Though there were laws against segregation, it was still the norm in the hearts and minds of many, especially in the church. In the churches of Christ, the strategy was to have a black church and a white church in the same town. At seminars, there was always a preacher from the "black church" to give one of the keynote speeches. Wyndham mentored and trained me just as he would have anyone else, not to be a  black minister, but to be a minister of the gospel who just happened to be black. Because of his influence, I was the first black man to be sent out to serve in the campus ministry in the churches of Christ, where diversity eventually became more the norm.

Breaking the Ineffectiveness Barrier

Wyndham, more than anyone, helped me overcome the areas that stood in the way of my effectiveness as a disciple. My sanguine temperament and conflict-avoiding nature were detriments to fruitfulness and impact. I wanted everyone to like me. Wyndham seemed to not care about that as he spoke the truth to me. He taught me the most valuable lessons in life and ministry—to put character and heart above

Wisdom Breaks Barriers

the outward appearance. The greatest battle in life is the battle to conquer self. More than in words, he demonstrated this in his life.

Recently when facing a challenging situation of major importance and consequence I could think of no better person to call to seek wisdom than my mentor, example, and best friend, Wyndham. He may now be physically disabled and retired from full-time ministry, but the life lessons he has taught me will never retire from my heart and soul.

For Reflection

Reflect on the level of courage you have to break through barriers. Are you willing to learn from others who are different than you? What barriers exhibited in your character might be hindering your effectiveness in helping people become Christians? Are you willing to ask hard questions that could create conflict? Does your life match the convictions you preach? Pray that God will help you be courageous in reaching needed breakthroughs in your life.

Father, thank you for breaking all barriers for me. Jesus, you gave your life to break the barrier separating me from God. How can I ever thank you? I will strive to thank you by the way I live. Make me aware of barriers that cause me to have any prejudices toward race, education, gender, looks, or social status so that I might repent of these. Please give me the courage to care more about what you think than what anyone else thinks.

WEDNESDAYS WITH WYNDHAM

*Father, please use me to break down barriers so that
more people can know you. Thank you, Father. Amen.*

12

WISDOM PERSUADES
AND IS PERSUADABLE

We all tend toward strong opinions on how some things should be done. We most often believe our opinion is the best way to do things. Ever been there? A better question: Have you ever had a day when you *didn't* feel opinionated about something?

We may have strong opinions about decisions made by leadership teams or at business meetings, or strong opinions with our roommates or spouse concerning the "proper way to place the toilet paper on the roll." (Just so you know, the paper goes down over the top.) We may have strong opinions on how to strategize while playing a game, or even deciding what is best to serve for a holiday meal.

We may have always done something a certain way or believe our ideas on how to do certain things have been thoughtfully and carefully discerned—and are right.

We may be right.

We may be wrong.

Or, we may be neither.

The more important outcomes for such disputable matters are preserving relationships, and that we "play well with others on the playground."

There are many different and acceptable ways to do

67

things that are not doctrinally mandated from the Scriptures. Yet it's so easy to wish others would just get on board with what we are sure is the best way to do a particular thing—which of course we believe is the right way.

Wyndham has, for years, practiced wisdom that understands the need to both persuade and be persuadable. Wisdom finds a way to reason together:

> Stop doing wrong,
>   learn to do right!
> Seek justice,
>   encourage the oppressed.
> Defend the cause of the fatherless,
>   plead the case of the widow.
>
> "Come now, let us reason together,"
>   says the LORD. (Isaiah 1:17–18a NIV1984)

We can either dig in our heels, insisting on our way, or we can seek to persuade and be persuadable. We can reason together.

Wisdom knows how to do the latter. So how do we persuade without being obnoxious? James 3:17 teaches us:

> But the wisdom that comes from heaven is first of all pure; then peace-loving, considerate, submissive, full of mercy and good fruit, impartial and sincere.

There is a way to persuade that proceeds from a pure heart. This way begins with prayer and the desire to do whatever is most pleasing to God, no matter how we are affected by a decision. Persuasion coming from a pure heart communicates this spirit through words, demeanor, body language, tone, and attitude. Humility or lack thereof is also visible. God resists the proud, and so do people.

Wisdom Persuades and Is Persuadable

All of you, clothe yourselves with humility toward
one another, because,

"God opposes the proud
but shows favor to the humble."
(1 Peter 5:5b)

While trying to persuade, pure hearts are also persuadable—because they listen and desire to learn. Because they value relationship over winning.

Peace-loving persuasion ensures that respect is given to other opinions and that condescending comments and gestures are avoided. Nothing undermines persuasion more than obstinance and disrespect.

We are more able to persuade when we speak with consideration to others—considering how our comments will be heard, considering our tone, considering our body language, considering where others are coming from. When we begin with a pure heart these attributes will naturally follow.

Wisdom knows that to persuade you must reason, come to the table with a pure heart, be considerate, and be humble. These same qualities allow us to be persuaded by another's thoughts as well. Wisdom is full of humility, with a willingness to be persuaded.

Wyndham, through wisdom that comes from God, has reminded me that it's okay to try to persuade (though I don't usually need much reminding). God calls us to seek to persuade others to follow him (2 Corinthians 5:11). In opinions, if we can persuade through a pure heart, consideration, and humility, it's all good. If we can't, we then get to practice humility.

In groups and in family life, I've seen Wyndham try

hard to persuade, and also have seen him be persuadable. And whatever the outcome, when he comes out of the arena of reasoning, he agrees to come out united. I have watched him when his opinion didn't "win the day" come out of the discussion with the mindset to be united with the group's decision in such a way that you would never know which way he leaned. (I would know, but you wouldn't.)

May we all gain wisdom to persuade and be persuadable.

For Reflection

Consider the ways you respond when you feel strongly about something. Would your friends or family members see you as one who calmly tries to persuade, or as someone who digs their heels in with little chance of being persuaded otherwise? Determine ways to practice being one who persuades rather than dictates.

> *Father, I praise you for your steadfastness. Your love and mercy are new every morning. Great is your faithfulness! Father, my steadfastness is often more like stubbornness. Help me be humble in my interactions, even when I feel strongly. Please help me to be quick to listen and slow to speak, interacting with humility. I need your wisdom to communicate with respect while trying to persuade, as sometimes I do need to be persuasive. Help me to know when to keep trying and when to let it go. Father, help me listen to hear. I want to be persuadable, which*

Wisdom Persuades and Is Persuadable

means letting go of past baggage and even traditions I hold dear. Let me, most of all, be persuaded by your word and the moving of your Spirit. Thank you for your patience, Lord. I long to hear you well. In Jesus' name, Amen.

13

WISDOM HAS VISION IN DARK TIMES

by Darryl Owens

Many years ago I needed to get together with Wyndham. I did not know I needed it, but he did, so he asked me to meet him at a popular coffee and sandwich restaurant. I had recently come out of the full-time ministry in Boston. I had also loudly and defiantly expressed my dissatisfaction with and toward the eldership of the Boston Church. So, yeah, we needed to get together.

We arrived around 10 AM. We stayed through the lunch rush and were headed toward dinner time. Wyndham mostly listened to me as I aired my grievances. With great patience, he helped, encouraged, and rebuked as needed.

Now we ask you, brothers and sisters, to acknowledge those who work hard among you, who care for you in the Lord and who admonish you. Hold them in the highest regard in love because of their work. Live in peace with each other. And we urge

Wisdom Has Vision in Dark Times

you, brothers and sisters, warn those who are idle and disruptive, encourage the disheartened, help the weak, be patient with everyone. Make sure that nobody pays back wrong for wrong, but always strive to do what is good for each other and for everyone else. (1 Thessalonians 5:12–15)

His rebuke appropriately stung as he reminded me of the biblical responsibility of the elders. He helped me see that they were men who had to make decisions for the good of the church. At one point, he leaned in and told me that I was spiritually out of line in my rebellion, criticism, and disrespect. I tried not to let it show, but I was a mess. I am sure Wyndham saw that my fight against leadership had become more important to me than my walk with God. And there I was with the one and only Wyndham Shaw, a man whose reputation for righteousness was well established. It was a bit intimidating and unnerving.

We stayed in that restaurant for so long that a manager came to our booth and told us we needed to buy more food or leave. As we were complying with the manager's direction Wyndham said to me, "One day when you are appointed an elder you will know exactly what I am talking about."

I laughed to myself and thought that he had no idea what he was talking about. My faith was at an all-time low. I had quit almost all forms of spiritual leadership and was just barely holding on. But this guy had vision for me. That was the fall of 2007. On October 19, 2016, I was appointed an elder in the Boston Church. May God grant me

even one-tenth of the impact, vision, and patience of
my dear brother, Wyndham Shaw.

*Darryl and his wife, Barbara, are an inspiring couple as
they give and serve in the church and the community. Darryl,
seeing a need for greater trust between police and youth,
began the Boston Police Teen Academy, which has become
a prototype for change. Barbara, who teaches in an inner-
city school, helped begin the Saturday Academy in Boston,
which helps at-risk youth find numerous avenues of support.*

For Reflection

Read 2 Corinthians 12:9–10. God, through his grace,
promises us that our weaknesses can become our strengths.
Therefore, we can boast of our weaknesses, since Christ's
power can be made perfect in them. Reflect on what you
see as your greatest spiritual weakness. Imagine what it
could look like in your life if this became a strength. Do you
believe that God can turn your weakness into a strength?
Share this with a trusted disciple and pray to this end,
knowing that God can transform you into his likeness, from
one degree of glory to another (2 Corinthians 3:18).

*Mighty God, I praise you that you made this incredible
world from nothing. You specialize in turning nothing
into something, and weaknesses into strengths. Father,
I easily see my weaknesses, at times feeling that I can't
change. Yet you tell me your grace is sufficient for every
need, including helping me to overcome my weaknesses. I choose to believe this. Give me the courage to
boast in my weaknesses, to be open and vulnerable with
you and others, allowing you to work to change me
from the inside out. I look forward to the day, Father,*

Wisdom Has Vision in Dark Times

when my weaknesses become strengths, to your glory. Fill me with faith and let me feel the power of your Spirit in me. To you, Father, be all the glory. Amen.

14

WISDOM BRINGS
A CALMING VOICE OF REASON

It's quite difficult to keep emotions out of difficult situations or conversations. Especially when we have been hurt. When we think something is unfair, we can easily become, in my friend Gordon's words, "wrapped around the axle." When this happens, our words produce turbulence rather than peace. A voice of reason calms. A quick tongue stirs up.

> Sin is not ended by multiplying words,
>   but the prudent hold their tongues.
> (Proverbs 10:19)

> My dear brothers and sisters, take note of this: Everyone should be quick to listen, slow to speak and slow to become angry, because human anger does not produce the righteousness that God desires. (James 1:19–20)

> A person's wisdom yields patience;
>   it is to one's glory to overlook an offense.
> (Proverbs 19:11)

I have long admired and learned from Wyndham's strong but calm posture in the face of difficult conversations and situations. Even amidst verbal attacks he reasoned, he listened, and he sought to keep a biblical

Wisdom Brings a Calming Voice of Reason

perspective—looking to what was right over who was right. When wrong, he was quick to apologize, but if biblical standards were clear, he was immovable. This came from his desire to live the righteous life that God desires above all else. He had to work hard and pray fervently to gain and maintain this posture and to overcome the temptation to become angry. He would be the first to tell you this.

Wisdom asks:

- Am I a calming voice of reason or an escalating voice of emotion?
- Do I seek a biblical perspective, or a perspective based on my opinions and feelings?
- Do my conversations build bridges or create chasms?

Bud Chiles recounts the importance of being a calming voice of reason, a peacemaker, and one who treats another with respect.

FROM LAWTON (BUD) CHILES:

Kitty and I had no idea what God had in store for us when we decided to move from Florida to New York in 1993. The move empowered changes in our marriage and the faith of our children for which we will be forever grateful. These changes occurred because God used people like Wyndham to inspire us, to instruct us in the ways of the Spirit, and to love and befriend us.

We got to know Wyndham and Jeanie well through our shared ministry work with HOPE *worldwide*. They led the New England and Europe work while we worked with HOPEww in Africa, the Caribbean, and the HOPE for Kids project in the US.

They were deeply experienced and wise leaders in our movement, and we were total rookies. But this fact did not color my relationship with Wyndham. From the get-go, he regarded me as a friend and treated me with respect. He actually wanted to learn from me! That meant so much to me, to have his deep friendship when I knew he far outpaced me in the fruits of God's Spirit.

I treasure all the talks we had that helped me reach a biblical perspective on the challenges we faced with our work and lives. He was always the calming voice of reason when there was disagreement about how to move forward with HOPE *worldwide* or how to resolve issues. He was and is a true peacemaker, and his spiritual talent in this area has been used to great advantage all over the Kingdom. To me, he seemed to have been born an elder, yet I knew he struggled as we all do.

The fellowship times with Wyndham were always so sweet. Fishing together on Woodpecker Pond, vacationing together in Puerto Rico. We are both Florida Gators, both love the outdoors, and both love God and his family.

What a fellowship! What a friend for life!

Blessed are the peacemakers,
   for they will be called children of God.
(Matthew 5:9)

Wisdom Brings a Calming Voice of Reason

May we all be calming voices of reason, treat each other with respect, and hold tight to a biblical perspective.

For Reflection

Ask yourself the following questions, and consider whether your roommate, spouse, children, and coworkers would agree:

- Am I a calming voice of reason or an escalating voice of emotion?
- Do I seek a biblical perspective, or a perspective based on my opinions and feelings?
- Do my conversations build bridges or create chasms?

Gracious Father, thank you that you are the same yesterday, today, and forever. I praise you for being slow to anger and abounding in love. Please, Father, help me to be more like you. Help me not to react in emotion but to be a peacemaker, thinking and acting with humility and gentleness. It is only in you and by your power that I can be a calming voice of reason. I believe you can make my weaknesses strengths as I depend on you. Thank you. In Jesus' name, Amen.

15

WISDOM KEEPS SHOWING UP

If Woody Allen had it right when he said, "Showing up is eighty percent of life," then Wyndham has lived a lot of life.

Showing up *consistently* is particularly important. Jesus did this. In fact, he promises to always be with those who follow him (Matthew 28:20). The early disciples, day after day, went into the temple courts and house to house, teaching and proclaiming the good news of Jesus (Acts 5:42). They showed up consistently, day after day.

It's one thing to show up, but showing up all the time requires a lot of love, determination, and self-discipline. I could always count on Wyndham to "show up," and this has made a great difference in his personal life, our marriage, our family, and our ministry. He has lived and taught the importance of this quality with his oft-practiced and oft-used phrase: "Set and kept times."

It's easy with today's busy and distracted lifestyles to live life flying by the seat of our pants, rather than living intentionally. Set and kept times have been an important part of Wyndham's life.

Wisdom Keeps Showing Up

The wisdom of the prudent is to give thought to
their ways. (Proverbs 14:8)

Most importantly, he set and kept times to walk and
talk with God. These weren't to fulfill a duty, but to fill his
soul. He counted on those times, as did I. There is nothing
more security-producing in my marriage than knowing my
spouse is spending time with his God. Thankfully and
amazingly, God always shows up and is always waiting for
us to show up—eager to spend time with us.

Wyndham also set and kept times for the two of us. To
pray together. To discuss how "we" were doing. To just
enjoy togetherness. Since our ministry consisted of long
days and nights, and we were always "on call," we set
aside Mondays to rest, to plan, to pray, and to enjoy nature. This wasn't just a nice idea, it was a necessity for us.
Mondays were carefully observed—set and kept.

He set times with each of the kids for heart-to-heart
communication, spiritual conversations, memory making,
and having fun. These were his most important "discipling"
times. The kids could count on some kind of individual
time with us each week. It wasn't easy once their schedules
grew when they hit their teens, but it was a priority, set and
kept. Dinner times were set and kept. At times these had
to be adjusted, but they could still be counted on.

Sharing "one-another" times with dear friends (Romans
12:10; 15:7; 15:14) were not just occasional happenings.
These were needed and important times for each of us that
we set in our schedules on a weekly, biweekly, or monthly
basis—in order to better practice "one-another" Christianity. Neither of us wondered if we would get together with a
particular person or couple, because the times were
guarded—set and kept.

As much as it depended on us, times were set and kept for hospitality. Wyndham suggested a practice we "set and kept" to make one night a week a time for hospitality in our home as we shared a meal, our lives, and the gospel with neighbors, friends, acquaintances, and those who had left the faith. This became our custom.

Set and kept times. These resulted in connection, security, friendship, growth, progress, vulnerability, and depth. The times certainly helped us, and prayerfully helped others as well. Because wisdom teaches us to keep showing up, we can continue to explore rare and beautiful treasures of deep spiritual friendships and relationships. These are available for anyone who builds their house with the wisdom of God.

> By wisdom a house is built,
>   and through understanding it is established;
> through knowledge its rooms are filled
>   with rare and beautiful treasures.
> (Proverbs 24:4–5)

For Reflection

Spiritual growth, outreach, relationships, and family-building do not accidentally happen. Think through your weekly and daily schedule. Do you set and keep plans to grow in these areas? If not, go through your calendar and plan ways you can intentionally begin a practice that leads toward growth in these areas. Give these plans to God in prayer and make the calls needed to set them in place.

Lord, thank you that you are a God of order. You planned from the beginning of time to give us what we need and so much more. You set the earth into orbit and

Wisdom Keeps Showing Up

put the stars in the heavens. You were deliberate as you gave covenants to your people and worked through history in order to, at just the right time, send yourself to us in Jesus. God, help me to have order in my life to wisely use the time you give me. Please help me be deliberate and consistent in times with my family, with my brothers and sisters in Christ, and with friends and neighbors and others I reach out to. Let my plans and times bring glory to you and help others draw close to you. Father, I commit these plans to you. Lead me by your Spirit to plan intentionally, staying close to you.

16

WISDOM UNDERSTANDS
BUCKETS AND FUNNELS

Nor'easters. They are fierce. For those of us living in New England, nor'easters mean high winds accompanied by hearty downpours of rain or hefty droppings of snow.

Today's forecast calls for a foot of snow. Last week's nor'easter was a rain event (where we live). That storm was unusually strong—an "every few decades" happening.

Two weeks ago we (for the second time) had our kitchen ceiling "repaired" from damage caused by a nor'easter a couple of years ago. Water had dripped through the ceiling and light fixtures, through the floor, and into the basement. This recent repair was done just in time for the past week's storm to undo all that had recently been fixed. (Actually, the repair only consisted of sanding and painting the ceiling, and obviously did not deal with the root [or roof] of the problem.) This storm re-damaged our ceiling—causing it to look just like it did before it was "fixed." The water once again leaked out of the ceiling through the floor and into the basement. I placed a bucket on the floor to catch the drips.

This unfortunate and true scenario reminds me of nuggets of wisdom Wyndham has often dispensed as he (and we) have worked with individuals, marriages, and families. He has referred to this lesson as "buckets and funnels."

84

Wisdom Understands Buckets and Funnels

In other words, the contents of the buckets that have been poured into us (by our families, our experiences, our hurts, our pains) will be funneled out from us to other receiving buckets (spouse, children, work associates, family members). When someone's toxic bucket (full of harmful and sinful patterns) is funneled into ours, we get hurt, and  then the contents of our own buckets can become rancid—filled with bitterness, envy, and all sorts of unresolved relationship problems and feelings. These, in turn, get funneled into others' buckets. This keeps on happening—unless we can stop the madness.

Wisdom knows we must each recognize what has been funneled into our bucket (both good and bad). We must then stop funneling and leaking harmful thoughts and practices into others' buckets. We can't just sand and paint over our buckets. We must fix or empty what's inside, find the root of the bad, and do repair work. We can't control what has been poured into our bucket, but we can control what is funneled out.

Toxic becomes pure only through the grace and forgiveness found in Jesus, and through the power of his Spirit to change our lives. He helps us to recognize the sludge and empty it from our buckets. Only then can we experience his healing forgiveness and refill our bucket with the fruits of God's Spirit. Then, when these purified and refilled buckets are funneled out, all kinds of good results are possible—and many lives are blessed.

How often I've listened as Wyndham has patiently

helped men and women discover what has (unintentionally) been filling their buckets and then spilling out and hurting others. He has helped them identify the poisonous contents, dump them out, and by God's power replace them with what is good, true, and right. Then they can pass on what is good and true and right.

The storms will continue to come. The water that goes through our roof and into our ceiling will come out, just as what goes into our bucket will funnel out. We can't just sand and paint over problems and expect our lives to be fixed. They must be repaired and changed from the inside out. The only lasting repair comes through Jesus and his words. He can empty our trash and fill our buckets with his treasures.

Since a big storm is coming, I will need to catch any leaks with a bucket until I discover the real problem. Meanwhile, check your bucket. The contents will be funneled into others.

> "No good tree bears bad fruit, nor again does a bad tree bear good fruit;
>
> for each tree is known by its own fruit. Figs are not gathered from thorns, nor are grapes picked from a bramble bush. The good person out of the good treasure of the heart produces good, and the evil person out of evil treasure produces evil; for it is out of the abundance of the heart that the mouth speaks." Luke 6:43–45 (NRSV)
>
> Create in me a pure heart, O God,
>   and renew a steadfast spirit within me.
> Do not cast me from your presence
>   or take your Holy Spirit from me.

Wisdom Understands Buckets and Funnels

Restore to me the joy of your salvation
and grant me a willing spirit, to sustain me.
(Psalm 51:10–12)
Therefore, if anyone is in Christ, the new creation
has come: The old has gone, the new is here! All this
is from God, who reconciled us to himself through
Christ and gave us the ministry of reconciliation.
(2 Corinthians 5:17–18)

FOR REFLECTION

Consider patterns that are difficult for you to break. Perhaps it is a tendency toward anger, people-pleasing, deceit, sinful patterns, addictions, self-abasement, fear of intimacy, being aloof, etc. Do you have any unfinished business from your past that is affecting your present? If the answer is yes, seek wise counsel to help you talk through the contents of your bucket. Get help learning how to empty your bucket and refill it with what is pleasing to God.

Gracious Father, I know I can't control what was put into my bucket, but I can choose how to respond, empty, and refill it. I know you are grieved by all evil that happens, and that deviations from your plan have brought on all kinds of dysfunctional consequences. I praise you that you are stronger than the evil one. Father, help me not to fear the clearing of my garbage. I cannot do this without you. Thank you for your Spirit and for your word. Thank you that you give me a spiritual family. Help me have the strength and confidence to be vulnerable, and please give me the wisdom to overcome. I pray along with David, "Create in me a pure heart, O God, and renew a steadfast spirit within me. *Do not cast me from your presence or take your Holy Spirit from me. Restore to me the joy of your salvation and grant me a willing spirit, to sustain me."* Amen.

17

WISDOM BREAKS THROUGH

Wyndham loved to speak of breakthroughs. He knew the importance of overcoming weaknesses. As I wrote chapters for this book, he at times was concerned that I painted him as "too good." I believe I did not, but nonetheless, he wanted to make sure readers knew he had flaws and was a sinner like everyone else. I said I would make sure to share the story about the wisdom of breakthroughs. I would tell him that I knew he wasn't perfect, but he was perfect for me. And he certainly set a high bar for righteousness. I never knew a more righteous man.

Breakthroughs are needed when a sin or character flaw simply does not change. You may experience a season of victory over the sin or bad habit, only to have it return with a vengeance, dogging your feet and filling you with discouragement. Do you ever feel like you need a "reset" button? A breakthrough? David needed a breakthrough to conquer the Philistines, who defeated the Israelites again and again. Likewise, we need breakthroughs to conquer the sins and character flaws that defeat us again and again.

> David inquired of God: "Shall I go and attack the Philistines? Will you hand them over to me?"
> The LORD answered him, "Go, I will hand them over to you."

89

> So David and his men went up to Baal Perazim, and there he defeated them. He said, "As waters break out, God has broken out against my enemies by my hand." So that place was called Baal Perazim. (1 Chronicles 14:10–11)

Baal Perazim means "break out" or "the Lord who breaks out." A breakthrough. In breakthroughs, God goes ahead of us and waits for us to show up. He shows up first. The question is, do we show up?

Wyndham grew up with seven siblings, and their behavior was often "controlled" by anger. It was seemingly easier to gain control by a raised voice producing fear and quick compliance, though rebellion often lurked inside. Our own stubborn sins or character flaws may stem from long-held habits resulting in a particular "default" behavior. We carry baggage into our lives from both learned behaviors and our own sinful desires. Though our marriage was strong, Wyndham would tell you (and did if you ever attended our marriage retreats) that he struggled with anger. Of course, I was the one who could most tempt him toward anger, so I felt it the most. He would not express it toward others. Oh, he never *physically* hurt me, but the tone of his voice could be loud and harsh. My response was to shut down, feeling hurt and fearful, which frustrated

Wisdom Breaks Through

him more. When the kids were older, one of our daughters began pointing his tone of anger out to him and told him he had five tones. When he got to the third one, she was afraid. I had been telling him similar things, and he finally heard it. I was serious. He made progress, but it was sporadic. Then he got serious.

He prayed fervently for a breakthrough. He read every scripture he could find on anger and asked the family to point out angry tones, and he willingly apologized and changed. He gave himself no excuse to become angry, putting on his heart James 1:19–20.

> My dear brothers and sisters, take note of this: Everyone should be quick to listen, slow to speak and slow to become angry, because human anger does not produce the righteousness that God desires.
>
> But the wisdom from above is first of all pure. It is also peace loving, gentle at all times, and willing to yield to others. It is full of mercy and good deeds. It shows no favoritism and is always sincere. And those who are peacemakers will plant seeds of peace and reap a harvest of righteousness.
> (James 3:17–18 NLT)

Wyndham sought godly wisdom, wisdom from above that is peace-loving, gentle *at all times,* and willing to yield to another. He took these verses to heart and committed them to prayer, to God, and to me.

He showed up with his conviction and desire, and God showed up to give him the power to change. This turned our relationship around. I was happy and so was he. His breakthrough was real. The Lord broke out the way for him as promised in 1 Corinthians 10:13:

> No temptation has overtaken you except what is common to mankind. And God is faithful; he will not let you be tempted beyond what you can bear. But when you are tempted, he will also provide a way out so that you can endure it.

Wyndham would then continue to share about this breakthrough journey. He would tell, with a loving smile, how after his breakthrough in overcoming anger that I had the nerve to ask him, "Now that you have quit becoming angry, do you think you could become kind and gentle in the way you speak to me?" I will never forget the look he gave me. At first it was a little incredulous, but it soon developed into a knowing acceptance. Wyndham then became kind and gentle in his conversations with me. He determined to change, asked God for the breakthrough, was vulnerable in asking for help, and was successful. I don't remember the anger. I remember the kind and gentle man who had a breakthrough. I am forever grateful to him, both for the change and for the example of gaining wisdom from above. This is a constant reminder to me that God can, as 2 Corinthians 12:10 states, turn our weaknesses into strengths.

FOR REFLECTION

What would you (or those closest to you) say is your besetting sin or weakness? Will you decide to have a breakthrough for change? If so, read applicable scriptures and put them on your heart. Ask God for a breakthrough

Wisdom Breaks Through

and open up to someone who can pray for you and ask about your progress.

> *Lord of the breakout, how can I ever thank you for your unfathomable power, love, and grace? Thank you that you go before me and have defeated the power of sin. I beg you to go before me as I break through _____. Give me the courage, perseverance, and conviction to stay the course and see this weakness become a strength. I cannot do this without you and depend on your Spirit to empower me to change. Thank you for your promise to be with me always. I love you forever. Amen.*

18

WISDOM
NEVER GIVES UP

This shirt is pregnant with meaning to me. No one knows (until now) the meaning behind this baby boy's outfit. It is a personal "stone of remembrance" for me, representing a time of desperation and faith—of disappointment and discovery.

The week of August 10, 2016, was full of hope and excitement for me and my family. My son and daughter-in-law would find out the gender of their third child, already having two girls. We prayed and fasted for God to give them a boy, and I was confident God would answer accordingly.

We also awaited a procedure that was thought to be a cure for Wyndham's then-undiagnosed disease. I envisioned taking down the wheelchair ramp and giving away all the medical mobility equipment we had acquired. I had no doubt God would answer this miracle prayer, as I never gave up. Sam and Leigh Ann would have their son, and Wyndham would be healed. I bought this little-boy outfit that says "Never Give Up" to give to them upon the news of a son. I had complete faith that God would answer both

Wisdom Never Gives Up

requests with a resounding "Yes." It made perfect sense. After all, God would be glorified.

However, the cupcakes in the gender reveal were pink, not blue. Wyndham's surgical procedure not only showed there was no cure after all, but brought on severe complications. He stayed in recovery for a very long time because the doctors thought he had suffered a stroke. Disappointment was thick—heavy with confusion. You see, I had never doubted. I never gave up. *What happened, God? I never gave up!*

Wyndham recovered from the surgery, but not the disease. I tucked the little outfit away, as I *still* believed God would surprise us at the baby's birth—the ultrasound would be wrong. "Never give up" would prevail! After all, we had been so disappointed with the surgery outcome; didn't we at least deserve blue cupcakes?

However, beautiful little Colette was born in December of that year. (Stay with me; we are forever grateful for sweet Colette and realize she is exactly who we wished for.) "Never give up" has taken on a new and much deeper meaning for me since that time.

I am reminded of this deeper meaning after long observing Wyndham's wisdom. Wisdom told him to never give up. I've seen him persevere through all kinds of adversity. I've watched him never give up when he was opposed for speaking the truth. I have seen him face deep discouragement and watched him never give up. I have seen him dismissed from a preaching job, with our baby on the way, no insurance, no place to go, and no savings—and never give up. I have heard him pray desperate prayers and never give up. I watched him believe that campuses and cities and neighborhoods were truly ripe for harvest and never give up. I have seen him believe in and counsel hurting marriages—and never give up. Now I see him barely able to talk, yet engage and share his love and convictions—and never give up. I watch him unable to do anything he once could do—and never give up. Many in his situation would have given up. He never will. He will live for whatever God has called him to do every day he is given, without giving up.

Yes, I bought this outfit to celebrate my victoriously answered prayers. I faithfully reasoned that if I never give up praying and believing, I will see God answer my desperate pleas. Those pleas were answered, just not how I had first hoped. Little Colette (Coco) was meant to be a Shaw. And now no one would ever wish it differently. She is the answer to our prayers, and we are all grateful.

As for Wyndham's illness...I can't say I am grateful, but I am surrendered, and I trust. I see God at work in mysterious ways. I believe God is able to heal him, but so far God has said no. I don't know why and may never know. Thus, "Never give up" takes on even greater meanings. When you are disappointed, never give up.

> We don't yet see things clearly. We're squinting in a fog, peering through a mist. But it won't be long before the weather clears and the sun shines bright! We'll see it all then, see it all as clearly as God sees us, knowing him directly just as he knows us!
> (1 Corinthians 13:12 MSG)

Whatever the circumstance, Wyndham hasn't given up, and neither shall I.

- When you are disappointed, never give up.
- As long as you have breath in you, never give up.

Wisdom Never Gives Up

- When you are doing good and are opposed, never give up.
- When you fail once again, never give up.
- When you can't see your way and things look hopeless, never give up.
- When you can't find an answer, never give up.
- When you think God hasn't heard you, never give up.

God is there and here. He is with us. He never gives up on us. Wisdom never gives up. Wisdom knows the reward that lies beyond disappointment.

So do not throw away your confidence; it will be richly rewarded.

You need to persevere so that when you have done the will of God, you will receive what he has promised. For,

"In just a little while,
    he who is coming will come
    and will not delay."

And,

"But my righteous one will live by faith.
    And I take no pleasure
    in the one who shrinks back."

But we do not belong to those who shrink back and are destroyed, but to those who have faith and are saved. (Hebrews 10:35–39)

But we're not quitters who lose out. Oh, no! We'll stay with it and survive, trusting all the way. (Hebrews 10:39 MSG)

No matter how tempted you are to quit, keep going. Crash through those quitting places. And never, ever give up.

Wisdom never gives up.

FOR REFLECTION

Consider times you have been disappointed. How has this affected your relationship with God? Reflect on ways God has been disappointed and knows how you feel. Know that he is with you during these times, and has a big-picture eternal plan that is far better than we can understand. We may never understand the "whys," and that's okay. Listen to some spiritual songs about trust, and find scriptures that can be your "go-to" scriptures when disappointment hits hard.

Faithful Father, how you longed for your creation to trust you and obey you. But they did not...and all evil broke loose. I can only imagine your disappointment, after providing multitudes of miracles and blessings with the Israelites, as they turned from you and worshipped idols. Father, your love amazes me as you watched this world kill your beloved Son and had to turn away. This puts my disappointment in perspective, but God, it still hurts. I know I can't see as you do. Father, help me to always trust your love and your big picture. God, help me to never shrink back, but to persevere. Thank you that you never give up on me. Let me feel the comfort of your love in the shadow of your wings. Amen.

19

WISDOM
LOVES TO FISH

by Jack Frederick

Fishing is not easy. If you don't love to fish, then fishing is often not fun; it's only fun when the fish are biting and you're catching fish. I never knew anyone who loved to fish like my friend Wyndham. Many times we drove at 4 am to Gloucester (Massachusetts) to fish from the jetty, a long rock wall fabricated from very large blocks of stone as a barrier to protect boats from sea waves.

We often took our sons Steven and Sam. Wyndham and Steven love fishing. Sam and I liked to go fishing when the fish were biting. By sunrise, I would lie sleeping on the huge rocks in the warm sun while Wyndham and Steven fished. Sam would entertain himself catching starfish with his bare hands in the shallow water.

Jesus promised his followers he would make them fishers of men. Many of them had been fishermen by trade; they probably liked fishing when they caught fish, since they could sell them and earn a living. Some, or at least Simon (Peter), demonstrated my "like for fishing" that day when Jesus was teaching by the shore. When Jesus asked him to put out to catch some fish, Peter grumbled, "We've been fishin' all night and haven't caught a thing...but if you say so we'll go fishing." They caught so many fish their nets began to break, and the boats began to sink (Luke 5:1–11).

Wyndham is that kind of fisherman. When others have been fishing all day and caught nothing, he can walk up and catch fish. Lots of fish. Big fish. I don't know how it works, I just like to go fishing with him…I catch fish too.

Wyndham is a fisher of people, like Jesus. He is good at that too, and I always liked doing it with him. I learned from him how to fish for people the way Jesus said we would. We caught lots of fish—big fish and little fish. Sometimes the nets got full; sometimes we had to call off our weekly Bible discussions where we invited visitors to come and learn because we had so many people individually studying the Bible to learn about Jesus that we didn't have time for Bible discussion groups. Besides, that's why you have Bible discussions, so you can encourage people to study the Bible and learn more about God.

Jesus knew Peter and his friends were fishermen. He knew they caught fish, at least sometimes. But he knew they needed to learn to love to fish, so he showed them how. And, in so doing, Jesus promised to teach them how to fish for people. These "unschooled, ordinary men" (Acts 4:13) learned from Jesus how to be good at fishing for people, and how to be effective. They learned to love it.

I'm not sure I could ever learn to love fishing, but I learned from my friend Wyndham to love fishing for people. I learned the value God placed on the men and women we taught to know him. I learned to be effective at fishing

Wisdom Loves to Fish

for people because God so values each person we help. The overwhelming reason I love doing it is that I feel such deep gratitude for the salvation God gave me through knowing him and his Son Jesus whom he sent (John 17:3).

The world desperately needs to know God. People face so many hardships and troubles. We read about them all the time in the news. We see politicians and leaders decry the pain, and they scramble to identify what they think causes problems in our society. Some things are evident, but at the heart of all this hardship is our need to know God and how he wants us to live.

We need more fishers who understand, more fishers with the courage to turn the world upside down. Whether we are "unschooled and ordinary" or well educated doesn't matter. We just need fishers with faith so that God can work powerfully in their lives to help others. We need fishers who love to fish, who love the people they are fishing for and want to rescue them from the darkness of this life.

I wasn't born loving to fish for people, I had to be taught...and I had to be willing to learn. The world is crying out for help. The people around you are crying out for help. You may think otherwise if you live in a religious place, as I do. In that case, pray for God to open your eyes to the need and to the harvest that is ripe on every  corner. The question is not how well you express yourself or how willing you are to speak, the question is: Are you willing to learn to love others as much as Jesus did? He said, "By this will everyone will know you are my disciples, because you love one another" (John 13:35).

For Reflection

Do you believe Jesus has called you to follow him and become a fisher of people? If so, what holds you back or distracts you from this purpose? How might you grow in your love for people and your courage to become a fisher for them? Ask God to renew your focus and purpose, and make a prayer list for those whom you long to see come to know Christ.

Father, thank you that Jesus continually called people to him, bringing us all hope and salvation. Father, please fill me with the same love for people that Jesus had. Help me to open my heart to them and see them through Jesus' eyes. Give me the love and courage to reach out, and Father, please lead me to open doors for your gospel. Make me aware and help me to have the right words to share with people what you have done for me. Amen.

20

WISDOM OFFERS
A SAFE PLACE

Do you remember being scared as a child and running to a parent's embrace? Or being caught in a storm and reaching the warm safety of shelter? Or have you sat white-knuckled on a turbulent airplane flight welcoming sweet relief as the wheels touched the ground?

Safe at last.

A safe place. An important place to find. A needed feeling to feel.

Without it, we are anxious, agitated, and afraid.

While God is our true safe place, when someone reflects his qualities, they offer an aura of safety, approachability, and confidence. A safety that is grounded in the safe place they have found in God. David understood this safe place:

> One thing I ask from the LORD,
>   this only do I seek:
> that I may dwell in the house of the LORD
>   all the days of my life,
> to gaze on the beauty of the LORD
>   and to seek him in his temple.
> For in the day of trouble
>   he will keep me safe in his dwelling;
> he will hide me in the shelter of his sacred tent
>   and set me high upon a rock. (Psalm 27:4–5)

WEDNESDAYS WITH WYNDHAM

Wyndham has oft been described, for good reason, as a safe place. When difficult situations arose, he has often been a person's first point of contact. When someone has needed help with a relational difficulty, he has been called on to help sort it out. When people were hurting, his integrity, his hugs, and the wisdom of his words have brought "safety" to many. He has provided a safe place for me, his kids, his grandkids, the church, and his neighbors and friends. (Only the fish aren't safe with him.)

> The evil of bad people leaves them out in the
>   cold;
>   the integrity of good people creates a safe
>   place for living. (Proverbs 14:32 MSG)

When I reflect on the ways Jesus, full of grace and truth, was a safe place, several encounters stand out to me. The Apostle John referred to himself as the one whom Jesus loved. The scene that unfolds in John 13 is quite incredible. Jesus, the creator of the world and the Son of God, was troubled. He shared his heart with his friends as they ate together.

John felt safe enough with Jesus to ask the obvious. He felt safe enough to lean his body against him. He felt the safety of assurance of Jesus' love for him.

> After he had said this, Jesus was troubled in spirit and testified, "Very truly I tell you, one of you is going to betray me."
> His disciples stared at one another, at a loss to know which of them he meant. One of them, the disciple whom Jesus loved, was reclining next to him. Simon Peter motioned to this disciple and said, "Ask him which one he means."

104

Wisdom Offers a Safe Place

> Leaning back against Jesus, he asked him, "Lord,
> who is it?" (John 13:21–25)

Jesus was vulnerable. He shared his heart. He shared meals. He sat on the floor with his friends. He gave affection. He told the truth.

In another instance, a crowd of religious law-keepers and leaders brought out a woman caught in adultery, intent on stoning her. As the account is given in John 8:1–11, we see Jesus' interactions both with the crowd and with the shamed and guilty woman. He treated her with dignity and did not side with the religious leaders. He offered grace (and truth). He reached the hearts, dispersed the crowd— and brought hope to the shamed woman.

Sometimes he spoke the truth while looking at someone with eyes that exuded love. Other times he called outcasts by name or made a point of touching them. Jesus wept. He was a safe place.

One of my friends, sitting behind us, took this picture during a church service a couple of years ago. I was not feeling well that day and rested my head on Wyndham's shoulder. On his other shoulder, our dear friends' special needs daughter rested her head. As Wyndham imitates Jesus, he offers a safe place.

What does a "safe place" look like? A safe place:

- Makes an individual feel loved, because they are loved
- Expresses affection
- Is vulnerable and approachable
- Shows respect

- Listens well
- Seeks to redeem, rather than condemn
- Validates one's value
- Doesn't assume the one who might appear "more religious" is right, but practices Proverbs 18:17
- Speaks the truth while leaving one full of hope
- Points to the ultimate safety, which is found in God alone
- Understands that we are living for something beyond this life

Wisdom offers a safe place.

FOR REFLECTION

What makes a place feel safe for you? Consider why God is the ultimate safe place and determine to go to him first for comfort and security. Reflect on how you may or may not be a safe place for others. How might you become more of a safe place, while still reflecting the truth of God?

Abba, Father, thank you that you are my safe place. Help me be completely open and vulnerable with you, as you already know my innermost thoughts. Hide me in the shadow of your wings and the cleft of the rock. In this security, God, I will be more able to be a safe place for others, leading them to you. Help me to show respect to all, to listen well, and to express love and affection for others. I depend on you for this ability, Father. You alone can keep me safe and secure. I thank you for your strength combined with compassion. I seek your face, and in you I find peace. Amen.

21

WISDOM BRINGS
RESOLUTION

Have you ever been in an awkward or difficult conversation and felt bad about it, yet never spoke of it again? It just dropped, as if it had never happened.

Or have you had a conflict and decided that silence is golden—and then placed the unresolved conflict in your museum of golden-silent-unresolved conflicts?

Or have you ever stored unresolved feelings in your heart? Then, a family member or friend asks if you are okay and you answer, "I guess. I dunno," and leave it at that.

Or have you asked your kids what happened in a certain situation, or asked them what was troubling them—only to receive a blank stare?

Nothing gets mentioned again. Unfinished.

The thought often prevails: *If I don't talk about it, it will just go away by itself.*

It rarely does. We store these little unresolved snapshots in our heads until they become full-blown photo albums in our minds. As a result, we feel weird with certain people, try to avoid them, or retreat into a cone of silence—our hearts unexposed. Unresolved.

Wisdom brings resolution to conflicts, unresolved feelings, and qualms. Wyndham had a commitment to bring anything unresolved to "real" resolution. Stating the obvious. Addressing the elephants parked in the living rooms.

Speaking the truth in love. In bringing resolution, he would open and close the discussions with a relevant scripture and heartfelt prayer.

He would ask the person(s): *What would resolution look like for you? What do you need in order to be resolved?* Then, conversations—with the backdrop of Jesus' heart and attitudes as the goal in mind—would begin. The conversations, however difficult, were to be honest; there could be no progress otherwise.

> The purposes of a person's heart are deep waters,
> but one who has insight draws them out.
> (Proverbs 20:5)

Words of resolution were always needed. He would ask: Are you resolved? The situation at hand would call for the question: *Does there need to be a heartfelt apology—as in actually verbalizing, "I am sorry. Please forgive me"?* If an apology is needed and given, is the apology accepted? For real?

"I dunno" was never an acceptable answer to "What's wrong?" This is a common answer, especially from kids to parents. Wyndham wouldn't force our kids to reveal what was going on in their hearts, but instead drew them out. This took time, and it took them having good experiences to convince them that he was a safe place. Creating a safe place comes from reassurance, a listening ear, the ability to relate, sharing how you understand or want to understand, vulnerability, and unconditional love. At times, "I dunno," is an excuse for not wanting to talk, while at other times the person may genuinely not know what is inside and need help figuring it out.

Wisdom Brings Resolution

Never let feelings linger unresolved. Unresolved feelings lead to bitterness. If you can't get something worked out, get help from a trusted (and spiritual) friend and adviser. Living rooms are much more livable when they are not inhabited by elephants. Vulnerability is hard, but it brings freedom from deep inside.  Jesus' words and principles are always true, such as in John 8:32—"the truth will set you free."

FOR REFLECTION

Is there anyone in your life with whom you are not resolved? What is needed for resolution, and how will you decide to proceed in order to get there? Clear the living room of all elephants.

> God of grace and truth, I praise you that you are fully grace and fully truth. Help me to grow in both. Give me the courage to speak the truth in love, and give me the grace to forgive. Give me the wisdom to know when and how to resolve my feelings with _____, so that there is nothing gnawing at my heart and no bitterness can take root. I know that the truth always sets us free. Thank you that I can entrust everything to you, who judges justly. Help me to grasp the meaning of the scriptures, "Love covers over a multitude of sins," and "Perfect love drives out fear." I rely on your love and courage to fill me. Thank you, Father. Amen.

22

WISDOM BELIEVES
"EVEN IF"

Do you ever contemplate the "what ifs" of life?

I do. All too often my mind turns simple happenings into dire circumstances. If I can't reach a loved one for a period of time, I'm certain they have been in a wreck or kidnapped. My fears can reach this conclusion far too easily. Can you relate?

Our thoughts explore many "what ifs." These thoughts often lead us to fear and lack of trust. I am sure God knows this about me; thus, he has proven to me time and again that he will be with me through anything. When I was making the decision to become a Christian, to give my life wholeheartedly to God, I asked myself several seemingly strange "what if" questions as I counted the cost of following Jesus:

> What if someone put a gun to my head and asked me to deny God? Would I boldly profess my faith?
> What if I was asked to move to Africa? Would I be willing to go?
> What if something horrible happened to someone I love? Would I still have something to give?
> What if…?

Shockingly, all of these "what ifs" have happened to me. There wasn't a gun to my head, but there was a knife

110

Wisdom Believes "Even If"

in my back. (If you want to hear this story, read *My Morning Cup*.) We were asked to move to Africa (and were eager to go) when plans beyond our control changed and we stayed. And now, the love of my life has a terrible disease.

Wisdom turns "what if?" into "even if."

When Wyndham learned the aggressive and progressive nature of his disease, he immediately read the book of Job and shared his thoughts as recounted, "Shall we accept good from God, and not trouble?" (Job 2:10b).

We believe God is good. God is love. No matter what. Even if.

Hard things happen throughout our lives. Continually. Just this week we experienced a time of angst in a difficult situation. I thought of many "what ifs," and Wyndham (in his wisdom) reassured me that God would take care of us. He always has. Providentially, we had just finished reading Hebrews 11 and 12 together. I gathered perspective as I remembered reading of faith heroes being sawed in two, accepting the confiscation of their property, and much more. Our problem dwindled in light of these scriptures. These faith heroes experienced many terrible "what ifs," and remained full of faith.

Wisdom changes our "what ifs" to "even ifs." This changes everything.

What if…we changed our "what ifs" into "even ifs?"

Consider carefully the "even ifs" (emphasis added) in these scriptures:

WEDNESDAYS WITH WYNDHAM

And when you and your children return to the LORD your God and obey him with all your heart and with all your soul according to everything I command you today, then the LORD your God will restore your fortunes and have compassion on you and gather you again from all the nations where he scattered you. *Even if* you have been banished to the most distant land under the heavens, from there the LORD your God will gather you and bring you back. (Deuteronomy 30:2–4)

"Please remember what you told your servant Moses: 'If you are unfaithful to me, I will scatter you among the nations. But if you return to me and obey my commands and live by them, then *even if* you are exiled to the ends of the earth, I will bring you back to the place I have chosen for my name to be honored.'" (Nehemiah 1:8–9 NLT)

Though a mighty army surrounds me,
　　my heart will not be afraid.
Even if I am attacked,
　　I will remain confident.

The one thing I ask of the LORD—
　　the thing I seek most—
is to live in the house of the LORD all the days of my
　　　life,
　　delighting in the Lord's perfections
　　and meditating in his temple. (Psalm 27:3–4 NLT)

Yet Jerusalem says, "The LORD has deserted us;
　　the LORD has forgotten us."

"Never! Can a mother forget her nursing child?
　　Can she feel no love for the child she has
　　　　borne?

Wisdom Believes "Even If"

But *even if* that were possible,
  I would not forget you!
See, I have written your name on the palms of my
    hands.
  Always in my mind is a picture of Jerusalem's
    walls in ruins." (Isaiah 49:14–16 NLT)

"For *even if* the mountains walk away
  and the hills fall to pieces,
My love won't walk away from you,
  my covenant commitment of peace won't fall
    apart."
The God who has compassion on you says so.
(Isaiah 54:10 MSG)

Shadrach, Meshach, and Abednego answered King Nebuchadnezzar, "Your threat means nothing to us. If you throw us in the fire, the God we serve can rescue us from your roaring furnace and anything else you might cook up, O king. But *even if* he doesn't, it wouldn't make a bit of difference, O king. We still wouldn't serve your gods or worship the gold statue you set up." (Daniel 3:16–18 MSG)

Jesus said to her, "I am the resurrection and the life; he who believes in Me will live *even if* he dies, and everyone who lives and believes in Me will never die. Do you believe this?" She said to him, "Yes, Lord; I have believed that You are the Christ, the Son of God, even He who comes into the world." (John 11:25–27 NASB)

True, some of them were unfaithful; but just because they were unfaithful, does that mean God will be unfaithful? Of course not! *Even if* everyone else is a liar, God is true. As the Scriptures say about him,

WEDNESDAYS WITH WYNDHAM

"You will be proved right in what you say,
and you will win your case in court."
(Romans 3:3–4 NLT)

Hold firmly to the word of life; then, on the day of Christ's return, I will be proud that I did not run the race in vain and that my work was not useless. But I will rejoice *even if* I lose my life, pouring it out like a liquid offering to God, just like your faithful service is an offering to God. And I want all of you to share that joy. Yes, you should rejoice, and I will share your joy. (Philippians 2:16–18 NLT)

But *even if* you suffer for doing what is right, God will reward you for it. So don't worry or be afraid of their threats. Instead, you must worship Christ as Lord of your life. And if someone asks about your hope as a believer, always be ready to explain it.
(1 Peter 3:14–15 NLT)

"Fear nothing in the things you're about to suffer—but stay on guard! Fear nothing! The Devil is about to throw you in jail for a time of testing—ten days. It won't last forever.
"Don't quit, *even if* it costs you your life. Stay there believing. I have a Life-Crown sized and ready for you." (Revelation 2:10 MSG)

These scriptures remind me that God is with me and loves me. Always and forever.

Even if.

Wisdom replaces "what if" with "even if."

114

Wisdom Believes "Even If"

FOR REFLECTION

Reflect on your biggest "what if" anxious thoughts. What would it look like in your thoughts and actions if you replaced your anxious thoughts with one of the "even if" scriptures? Commit one of the scriptures to memory.

Faithful Father, I confess my fears and my desire to be comfortable. Help me to remember your faithfulness throughout history and in my life. Grow my heart to have the courage and faith to rely on your love and your wisdom, especially since I cannot see the big picture as you can. Thank you that you hold the future and have included me in that plan. In Jesus' name, Amen.

23

WISDOM FINDS
GOD'S PRESENCE

Me shaving Wyndham and him laughing at me doing the facial contortions that he would do, even though he now can't

Wyndham laughed as I shaved his face. (He can no longer use his hands, so he relies on me for all types of personal hygiene.) He laughed, because as I shaved his face, I made all the facial contortions that he would have made had he been shaving himself. I thought about this as it relates to holiness (I know, my mind is weird.) Because I have observed him and studied his face, I imitated, without thinking, the expressions he would make. Likewise, when one becomes familiar with the "face" or presence of Jesus, their actions express who he is, what he would do, and how he would think.

Wyndham has consistently set an example for me by seeking God's presence in prayer. You see, prayer is not merely something we do to check off our spiritual activities for the day. Prayer is dependence on God. Prayer is desperation. Prayer is relationship, presence. Prayer is trusting. Wyndham likes to begin and end the days with prayer.

Wisdom Finds God's Presence

He would begin vacation times with prayer, begin car rides with prayer—even fishing trips with prayer. When he would visit with someone, he would ask to pray with them, and when someone visits us, he wants to pray with them. He would seek God's face, to better know him.

We began praying with our kids when they were newborns, and we still pray with them. We love to pray with our grandchildren, because we, like their parents, long for them to know the presence of God.

One of our favorite scriptures is in Exodus 33. Moses is faced with the "I don't know what to do or where to go" dilemma. So—he prays.

> Moses said to the LORD, "You have been telling me, 'Lead these people,' but you have not let me know whom you will send with me. You have said, 'I know you by name and you have found favor with me.' If you are pleased with me, teach me your ways so I may know you and continue to find favor with you. Remember that this nation is your people."
>
> The LORD replied, "My Presence will go with you, and I will give you rest."
>
> Then Moses said to him, "If your Presence does not go with us, do not send us up from here."
> (Exodus 33:12–15)

Wisdom knows that when God's presence is with us, we will be okay.

If God's presence is not with us, we can have all kinds of fabulous or not-so-fabulous ideas and plans...but we had best not move forward.

God with us, God's presence, God's wisdom—is everything.

I took this picture a few nights ago because it's a common scene. Whenever Sam comes (a couple of times a week) to help with some of the routines like getting Wyndham into bed, this is a familiar scene—Sam praying with his dad the last thing at night. (I have also learned that Sam and our daughters pray by phone together very early in the morning once a week.) No one asked them to do this. They have learned wisdom because they need God's presence in their lives.

We can't fix our situation. We don't know what to do. But our eyes are on him.

God's presence is what really matters.

FOR REFLECTION

What does God's presence mean to you? How might you more keenly feel his presence in your life? Consider the habit and practice of prayer in your life. Do you see it as a spiritual activity for a Christian, or is it a desperately needed relationship time for you? Consider that God looks forward to being with you as well and determine to take time to be still with God, learning more of what it means to be in his presence.

> *Father, you know all things. You are wisdom personified and always want what is best for me, even if I must go through difficult times. Thank you for going through these times with me. I don't want to go forward without your presence, Father. Help me know more what it means to seek your face more fully, and may your presence transform my thoughts and actions every day. Keep this desire in my heart that I may seek you above all. In Jesus' name, Amen.*

24

WISDOM
IS "WHATABURGER"

by Sheridan Wright

I know that this title sounds weird...but bear with me. I have enjoyed reading chapters in *Wednesday Wisdom with Wyndham* and hearing others recount how Wyndham, in God's wisdom, has had an impact on their lives. My reaction is always the same: no surprise. I smile to myself and think, "Yep, that's Wyndham!"

Back to Whataburger. I entered the University of Florida as a freshman in the fall of 1972. Wyndham was the Resident Assistant on my dorm floor. As was his custom, he invited me to the "soul talk" (small group Bible discussion) in his room on Monday nights.

You know how some people enter college with lofty goals of high achievement and a focused dedication to accomplishing these goals? Well, I was *not* one of those people. I had a passion for foolishness, and it seemed to come to me with gift-like ease. Yet the soul talk intrigued me. Initially, I went, not because I was searching, but because of Wyndham's sincerity of faith—he had neither the self-righteousness nor the weirdness that I had witnessed in many others with devout belief. During the next two months, I developed a love-hate relationship with the "soul talk." I loved

119

the practicality and relevance of the Bible, but I hated the way it unnerved me. The unnerving won out, and I quit going. Two months later, after a night of "drinkin' and druggin'"—in an act of sheer stupidity—I fell three stories off a dormitory roof.

Because I had partially separated my hip in the fall, my mobility was restricted, and I was limited to my dorm room for a few days of recovery. A knock sounds at my door—in walks Wyndham. Now keep in mind that by this point in time, I had not been to soul talk in a couple of months; I was plunging headlong in the opposite direction of everything Wyndham had tried to get me to understand. I did not want to know what the Bible said. I was trying to forget what I had already learned; and to top it all off, my best thinking had led me to a dorm room convalescence from a near-fatal incident.

If ever there was a prime time for a sarcastic remark like "Attaboy Einstein, you proud of yourself?" this was it. Instead, Wyndham said, "Sheridan, I'm going to Whataburger, can I bring something back for you?" At first sound, this may seem quite trivial—an insignificant tidbit of information. Yet, if that is so, then let me pose this question: Why do I remember it forty-four years later as if it were yesterday? I knew I was a fool—I had proved it scientifically. I was in the crosshairs of ridicule and condemnation. I was running from God. I was running from Wyndham. I was running from anyone who had anything to do  with God or Wyndham. Yet, what did I get? An act of service…an act of grace.

Wisdom Is "Whataburger"

To me, wisdom is not so much the accumulation of knowledge, it is the right use of the knowledge you have. Wyndham knew Jesus, he knew God's word, and he knew his fellow man. To be sure, there are times when you have to confront, times when you have to forthrightly speak the truth. Wyndham does not shy away from that. Yet in that dorm room, all his knowledge of Jesus, God's word, and human beings caused him to give this guilty soul an act of grace. In doing this, he gave me a foretaste of a biblical truth that one day would define my life: "But God demonstrates his own love for us in this: While we were still sinners, Christ died for us" (Romans 5:8).

Is it any wonder that six months later, when I came to my senses and wanted to get my life right with God, I would want to find Wyndham? By that time I was living off campus and did not know where he was. I prayed that God would allow me to find him. The very next day I ran into him right in the middle of a campus of 24,000 students. Within a week I was baptized into Christ—on January 13, 1974.

I suppose that the nutritional merit of a Whataburger is a matter of debate. I can neither affirm nor deny it. But one thing I do not doubt: to have the wisdom of Christ is to reach out to individuals with genuine concern and to say or do the right thing at the right time. Wyndham did that. Wyndham taught me that. Wyndham is that.

Thank you, my brother and my friend, for showing me the Way. Thank you for that "Whataburger mission of mercy" that just confirmed what I had witnessed my freshman year in Jennings Hall—you *really* believe, you *really* follow Jesus, and you *really* care about the glory of God and the salvation of people. I love you and I gratefully owe you a debt of love...my wife, my children, and my grandchildren owe you a debt of love.

If I let my imagination go, I picture all of us at the judgment giving an account of our lives. For many of us, the name Wyndham Shaw would come up in that account. *He led me to you; he helped my marriage, my parenting; he cared enough to rebuke; he shepherded me; he brought me a burger...*

As we continue, the Lord smiles, "Yep, that's Wyndham—well done, good and faithful servant!"

FOR REFLECTION

Consider someone you are reaching out to who perhaps has not responded the way you may have prayed they would. Determine and plan an act of grace you can show them.

Lord, help me to practice compassion and deeds of kindness. I know I never know who might respond to you through the grace I bestow on them. I can only do this because you are a God of grace and have shown me unimaginable grace. Let me be alert to ways to serve people, even in small gestures. I desire to do this, but I confess I get busy and distracted. Help me be open to the prompting of your Spirit. Amen.

25

WISDOM KNOWS
A Secret

It's a typical morning.

C-Pap mask off. ✓ Contoured pillows under legs removed. ✓ Ice packs under elbows moved. ✓ Foam boots (to prevent pressure sores) pulled off. ✓ Pulled from bed onto power chair. ✓ Teeth brushed. ✓ Face washed. ✓ Shaved. ✓ Dressed. ✓ (All done for you, not by you) Picked up and put on portable commode. ✓ Back on chair. ✓ Help eating breakfast. ✓

And so the day begins.

My morning question to Wyndham: *So, how are you today?* His answer, each day: *Good, I'm good.* And he means it. He is grateful for this day (as am I). I then put his shirt on him (almost always a Life is Good T-shirt because they are comfortable, easy to get on and off, and have a good message). Today's shirt reads, "LIFE IS NOT EASY. LIFE IS NOT PERFECT. LIFE IS GOOD." Shirt on. That works. ✓

WEDNESDAYS WITH WYNDHAM

We share thoughts, usually some laughter, and a prayer. A prayer for "daily bread." In that prayer, we share a secret.

Wyndham has a secret.

Wisdom knows the secret.

The secret is this:

> I know what it is to be in need, and I know what it is to have plenty. *I have learned the secret* of being content in any and every situation, whether well fed or hungry, whether living in plenty or in want. I can do all this through him who gives me strength. (Philippians 4:12–13, emphasis added)

> This message was kept secret for centuries and generations past, but now it has been revealed to God's people. For God wanted them to know that the riches and glory of Christ are for you Gentiles, too. And *this is the secret: Christ lives in you.* This gives you assurance of sharing his glory. (Colossians 1:26–27 NLT, emphasis added)

Christ in you (and me). This is the secret—a secret that envelops our very being. A secret that proves true day after day; however, since these verses have been read for nearly 2,000 years by countless people, it's really no secret. Unless Christ doesn't live in you. Then true joy, abiding peace, and solid hope seem unattainable...a secret only longed for.

This secret remains a mystery of sorts. How else could Wyndham be "good?" How can we be deeply happy, despite his really tough situation?

It's because of the secret.

Wisdom Knows a Secret

"Christ in us" is unable to be physically seen or touched. It's a secret to the physical three- dimensional world in which we live; nonetheless, it's real. When we have Christ in us, the secret is revealed.

What does it mean to have Christ in us? It means we have the same power in us that raised Jesus from the dead. Do we hope for a miracle? Absolutely. But have we both already overcome death through Christ in us? The answer is a resounding "Yes."

This secret means that God pours his love into our hearts through his Holy Spirit (Romans 5:5). We can feel loved because we are. We can give love because God keeps pouring it into our hearts. It doesn't run out even if we are tired or our bodies don't work.

I have no other explanation as to why we can approach each day with joy, gratitude, and hope except for God's Spirit living in us. And these are realities, not wishful thoughts.

The secret of Christ in us means that no matter the circumstances, we can have a deep joy, an abiding peace that doesn't make sense, and a hope that can't be crushed.

> May the God of hope fill you with all joy and peace as you trust in him, so that you may overflow with hope by the power of the Holy Spirit. (Romans 15:13)

God's Spirit is Christ in me. In us. Meditate on this. All the power of Christ. All the love of Christ. All the peace of Christ. The whole purpose of Christ—really and truly living inside me—the part of me that can't be touched but is eternal. The soul.

This is wisdom's secret.

For Reflection

Plan some extra time to meditate on ways Christ *in* you changes you. Do you not only know about him, but do you *know* him? Take time to be still, perhaps singing or listening to hymns or worship music. As you read the Bible, pause and let God speak to you, and pray to experience his presence. If you have difficulty connecting with God, ask yourself if perhaps unrepented and unconfessed sin, continual busyness, or distractions may be keeping you from experiencing Christ in you.

Abba, Father, I stand amazed that you know me from the inside out and that you love me. I pray that you are always enough for me and that I will delight in your presence. Let me listen to your word and be attentive to your Spirit. I long for the peace that only you can give. Help me to rid myself of anything that stands in the way of connecting with you. In Jesus' name, Amen.

26

WISDOM CONNECTS

Anyone can say words; however, wisdom can turn words into connections. Without connection, it's impossible to communicate on a heart-to-heart level. Wisdom connects words to the heart.

Wyndham, for as long as I have known him, has been a great connector. As he connects deeply with individuals, he also helps them connect with each other. Connectors do this. Their connections are contagious. If the connection is only  with us, we build dependence instead of family. For years, I have studied Wyndham's ability to connect and have sought to emulate this gift as much as possible.

Ironically, Wyndham's body has a major connection problem. Though his mind is excellent, and his body *should* be physically able to function, it doesn't. There's a disconnect. It is as if a drawbridge has gone up between his brain and body. They no longer connect well. Our nervous system normally does this connecting automatically; but, unfortunately, this connection is now missing for him.

Too often, the metaphorical drawbridge goes up when

people try to connect. Words are spoken but they don't bring about closeness or desired unity. They simply give information.

I've noticed several aspects of connection as I've "studied" Wyndham's ability to connect. This connection comes not just from words said, but also from the emotional atmosphere and feelings that surround the words. These bring down the drawbridge so that connections can be made. I have watched him exude the following attitudes, which result in true connection:

- **You are important to me. I care about you and I value you.** This attitude is a bridge between spoken words and our understanding. The drawbridge is down when we know people care as they speak to us. Even now, though Wyndham can barely talk, he will ask, "Did you give them my love?" or, "How did her meeting go?" or, "Did Caleb catch a fish today?" Because he cares.

- **I want to hear what you have to say.** We all want to be heard and understood. We communicate this when we truly *do* want to hear what others say. This invites connection.

- **I will be vulnerable.** People connect to our weaknesses. It's often humbling to share them, but we can likely think of people we have easily connected with because of their vulnerability. Sometimes (often) these chapters feel vulnerable. I always read them to Wyndham and ask if it's okay to share. He continually tells me that he knows that connection is in the vulnerability.

Wisdom Connects

- **I want to have eye-to-eye contact with you.** Often a look from Jesus elicited connection and emotion. Truly the eye is the lamp of the body, as Jesus stated (Matthew 6:22). There's just something about eye-to-eye connection that helps beget heart-to-heart connection.
- **I want to hug you.** Have you ever been speaking to someone and their kindness and connectivity just make you want to get up and hug them? Wyndham knows the importance of affection. We all need hugs. More than we think. Lots of them. It's hard to hug someone and stay disconnected.
- **I will be honest with you and I want you to be honest with me.** There's nothing like the truth that brings the freedom that allows connection. As Proverbs 24:26 (NLT) states, "An honest answer is like a kiss of friendship."
- **I want to leave you encouraged and hopeful.** No matter how difficult a situation or conversation, we connect to those who can offer hope (which is always found in Christ). I have noted that Wyndham gives hope even (and especially) in difficult situations and conversations.
- **I want to be approachable.** I'm always inspired by the way Jesus easily connected with children and the poor. He was/is the greatest leader ever, but easily approached by what others considered "the little (or less important) people." We must make extra effort to ensure that others feel comfortable approaching us.

129

How can we ever connect with someone we can't easily approach?

I'm so grateful that Almighty God encourages us to approach him (Ephesians 3:12; Hebrews 4:16). May we all grow in wisdom to connect as we speak and engage with others.

FOR REFLECTION

Think of someone with whom you easily connect. What qualities make this connection easy? Do you reflect these same qualities in your interactions with others? Consider one quality that you will decide to grow in to enable you to connect more easily with others.

Father, thank you that you have broken the barriers that separate us from you. It is extraordinary that you, who hold the universe together, desire to connect with me. Help me reflect this love, approachability, vulnerability, and humility so that my life can help others see and connect with you. Please help me to connect with you and with others on a deep, heart level. In Jesus' name, Amen.

27

WISDOM
Is Mind Change

by Gordon Ferguson

This chapter title will remind many of you of an excellent book written by Tom Jones about how he came to view and deal with multiple sclerosis. It is a most encouraging and inspiring book and one that I imagine Wyndham and his family have received much help from as they deal with his debilitating disease. But this chapter is about the abundant godly wisdom possessed by Wyndham, and so we are discussing other aspects of mind change.

Changing our minds is not often an easy task. It is not science but much closer to an art form. Many questions asked and answered about mind change tell us a lot about a person. How quick are we to change our minds—too quick or too slow? What causes us to change our minds—emotions or clear reasoning? Who influences us most to change our minds—those closest to us or those who make the most sense? What is our attitude about changing our minds—willingness or begrudging reluctance? What motivation is strongest regarding changing our minds—a desire to be right or seeking to determine truth? Good questions, don't you think?

The whole process of mind change is demonstrated extraordinarily well by Wyndham. I've watched him in this

131

process many times in many circumstances with many people. He has mastered the process in a way that few have, providing us with yet another lens through which to observe his wisdom.

Wyndham is a slow thinker in one sense—not caused by a limitation of intellectual powers at all, but by a self-imposed spiritual limitation. He simply refuses to rush into judgment. I have known many leaders in the church who prided themselves on being able (in their minds, at least) to size up situations and make quick decisions. Many times these decisions were made after hearing only one side of a story (often a friend's or another leader's side), and many times the lives of others were significantly affected by their kneejerk decisions. Just thinking about the occasions when I observed this process in the past gives me a pit in my stomach right now. Had those types of self-assured, cocky, arrogant decision-makers not read the Bible?

My dear brothers and sisters, take note of this: Everyone should be quick to listen, slow to speak and slow to become angry. (James 1:19)

The one who has knowledge uses words with
    restraint,
and whoever has understanding is
    even-tempered. (Proverbs 17:27)

Do you see someone who speaks in haste?
    There is more hope for a fool than for them.
(Proverbs 29:20)

The first to present his case seems right,
    till another comes forward and cross-examines.
(Proverbs 18:17)

Wisdom Is Mind Change

Wyndham is an exceptionally patient and careful listener. He won't interrupt a person sharing their heart—and he won't let others interrupt them either. I know—I've been in both places with him! He and Tom Jones remain two of my most trusted confidants, the two men whose counsel I cherish most. After leaving Boston years ago, I have flown back there on several occasions primarily just to get time with Wyndham and have him talk me off the ledge. He not only knows how to change his mind toward the right direction, but he can help others do that in a masterful way.

He changes his own mind by time-tested biblical and practical principles. He is not quick to change his mind, but he does understand the time-sensitiveness of some decisions. Unlike some leaders I have known, he is not afraid to make decisions because of worrying about being wrong or worrying about possible reactions or responses. He just wants to make righteous decisions, not necessarily popular ones. His quest for truth drives him, and he is never satisfied with *good* or *better* when *best* is within reach.

His mind changes are seldom emotionally based, but are based on those principles mentioned above that fit the situation most clearly. That being true, the emotions of others are not weighed much in the final decision, although they are respected and listened to carefully leading up to that decision. His wisdom in changing his mind and the minds of others leads him into answering all the questions raised in the second paragraph in the right way. He is never overly influenced by who is speaking, but rather by what is being said. Neither favoritism nor sentimentality will carry the day with him. *What* is right is the clear target and not *who* is right—himself or anyone else in the discussion.

As all the chapters in this book show, Wyndham's wisdom is demonstrated in many, many ways. But in my judgment, it is shown perhaps best in the realm of mind change—his own and that of others through his direction. He is not only at the top of my list when seeking  guidance in the most serious life matters, but at the top of my wife's list as well. He earned that spot soon after our arrival in Boston in 1988 by carefully guiding us through our needed mind changes about our marriage and ministry. I don't think I would have survived the ministry part without him, and I know that our marriage would not have become what it has without him. Mind change, the fine art of discovering the pinnacle of spiritual thinking, is sought by many but mastered by few. Wyndham Shaw is one of the few.

For Reflection

Think about your communication. Would those close to you say you are quick to listen and slow to speak? If not, what can you do to grow as a listener? Determine to consciously listen well, without formulating your next response. Pray to be one who can listen with principle-based emotions rather than feeling-based sentiments.

Wisdom Is Mind Change

Lord, thank you that you are described as a man of integrity who pays no attention to who others are, but you speak the truth in accordance with God. Help me to listen and speak with integrity, more concerned for your grace and truth than for my point of view, right or wrong. I ask for your Spirit to help me be quick to listen and slow to speak, that I might hear well and respond in love according to what is right. Thank you for those in my life who help me to grow through my weaknesses. Amen.

28

WISDOM
Loves to Laugh

Each night lately I read aloud from the Bible and then we pray. Wyndham can't hold a book, and reading is too tiring for him. Last night as I was reading, I verbally stumbled with a tongue-twisting word. I kept saying it wrong, repeating it and saying it wrong again. Wyndham's voice is weak, but as I was reading, tongue-twisted, this quiet voice came from the man lying in the bed who almost looked as if he was asleep... "Easy for you to say."

My concentration completely left me when I heard this. I laughed for a while at his quick and sarcastic comment.

We laugh a lot. We need to. We encounter a lot of daily (hourly) hard things in our lives during this stage of our lives. We can cry or laugh. Occasionally we cry, but most often we choose to laugh. We intentionally laugh and find things to laugh at. Laughing is good for our health. And, it feels better. It even helps Wyndham clear his lungs.

Mayo Clinic reports that laughter induces physical changes in our bodies. It stimulates our heart, lungs, and muscles and increases our endorphins. Laughter also activates and relieves our stress response, soothes tension, improves our immune system, relieves pain, increases personal satisfaction, and improves our mood.[1]

1. http://www.mayoclinic.org/healthy-lifestyle/stress-management/in-depth/stress-relief/art-20044456

Wisdom Loves to Laugh

Ecclesiastes 3:4 tells us that there is "a time to weep and a time to laugh, a time to mourn and a time to dance." I am quite sure God has a sense of humor. Just look at some of his creations! The porcupine, the aardvark, the otter, the penguin, puppies, and the sloth likely induce some heavenly laughter. I even follow an Instagram post that has the sole purpose of showing the cuteness and funny antics of animals. Think of some of the crazy and unlikely ways God has worked in your life. Certainly, some of these show God's sense of humor (as along with his incredible grace toward us).

I find remarkable irony and humor (and God's wisdom and power) when in Numbers 22 Balaam's donkey spoke like a man and Balaam, well, he acted like a donkey. And picture when Gideon's tiny army defeated the Midianites by blowing rams' horns and breaking clay jars (Judges 7). And Jesus, God in the flesh, was born in a stable, was presented as a king riding on a donkey, and his lineage included Rahab, a prostitute.

Likely, since we don't live in the first century, we miss much of the humor of Jesus as he uses hyperbole, parables, and exaggeration to make his points. *The Dictionary of Biblical Imagery* says, "Jesus was a master of wordplay, irony, and satire, often with an element of humor intermixed."[2]

Consider Jesus' word pictures of a log in someone's eye and religious leaders straining at gnats and swallowing camels. Swallowing a camel?

But most convincingly, we are created in the image of God! You are, and I am too—and I sure do love humor. I

---

2. Leland Ryken, James C. Wilhoit, and Tremper Longman III, eds., "Humor—Jesus as Humorist," *Dictionary of Biblical Imagery* (Downers Grove, IL: InterVarsity Press, 1998), 410.

love to laugh. It's one of my all-time favorite things to do.

The proverbs of wisdom recount the benefits of a joyful disposition. This would certainly include smiles and laughter. The Scriptures knew this long before Mayo Clinic found out.

> A cheerful heart is good medicine,
>   but a crushed spirit dries up the bones.
> (Proverbs 17:22)

Proverbs also adds, "A happy heart makes the face cheerful" (15:13); or seen from a different view in verse 30, "A cheerful look brings joy to the heart" (NIV1984). Proverbs 16:24 tells us, "Pleasant words are a honeycomb, sweet to the soul and healing to the bones."

It's good to laugh. To be cheerful. This sign hangs in the entrance to our living room, and it's a good one.  (And yes, the Red Sox playing in the background adds joy as well.) While Wyndham takes a small amount of medicine for some symptoms, the best medicine is a cheerful heart.

May we all heed the wisdom of God (and this sign) as we "Live well, laugh often, and love much."

FOR REFLECTION

As you go about your day, take extra notice of God's creation and find some of the humor in even the small things. Deliberately smile more today than you normally do and consider how that affects your emotions. Pray to be a cheerful person.

Wisdom Loves to Laugh

Father, thank you that in the seriousness of life, you made animals and insects that truly do make us smile. Thank you for the infectious smiles of babies and children. Help me to be positive and cheerful as I interact with others, exuding the joy that you give me through your Spirit. Thank you that you have overcome sin and death and are the giver of life and hope. Help me to reflect this life, hope, and joy in my attitude.

29

WISDOM CLINGS
TO THE ROCK

It seems the weather has been particularly wild all over the world. Last week many of our friends in the Carolinas were dealing with a hurricane. Today we got the remnants—torrential downpours and fierce thunder and lightning. Ours only lasted a day. Theirs lasted several days, and many are still underwater. In other places all over the world, people are still picking up pieces after storms, with homes destroyed and streets flooded. Homes on the sand near the oceans have little hope of standing.

For as long as I can remember, Wyndham, when he could still speak well and pray out loud, would thank God for being his rock. He always used this term. I don't think I appreciated this metaphor nearly as much then as I do now.

Most weeks, when the weather allowed, we would walk and pray at our special place about forty minutes from our home, in a town called Manchester-by-the-Sea. We would walk a trail leading to a place so beautiful it seemed unreal. At the end of the trail we approached an expanse revealing a most stunning panoramic

Wisdom Clings to the Rock

view of the rocky North Atlantic shore. Before we neared the end of the trail approaching this gorgeous view, we would pass a gigantic marble rock. It has likely been sitting on this hill overlooking the ocean for centuries. This  solid rock has withstood years of crashing waves and howling nor'easters.

I always admired the rock and thought it was such a great addition to an already priceless view. It provides even more ambiance. I admire the strength and beauty of this rock, but I have never had the need to hold on to it for dear life. Now, as the winds and waves of deteriorating health howl, Wyndham's (and my) true rock, Jesus, means everything to me. The solid rock of Jesus is no longer something I just admire; everything in me depends on it. This rock is clung to, sat on, and is essential in every way.

Because our rock is the unchanging, all-powerful, and loving God who has been a friend for many years, Wyndham's faith, joy, and peace are unshakable. He has the wisdom to hold to the rock, to sit on the rock, to hug the rock, and to never leave the rock. This rock enables him to have patience and perseverance, even while suffering through an extremely difficult season of life. Without this rock, we would surely have been swept away, torn apart by the waves.

Because the rock is solid, and he has the wisdom to hold on, he is okay. We are okay. We are better than okay; we are very blessed. Sometimes sad, but secure in hope. The view from the rock is always spectacular, even in a storm. Perhaps especially during a storm.

Everyone needs this rock, for it can withstand any storm. It's not meant to merely be viewed but is meant to be embraced.

> Hear my cry, O God;
> listen to my prayer.
>
> From the ends of the earth I call to you,
>   I call as my heart grows faint;
>   lead me to the rock that is higher than I.
> For you have been my refuge,
>   a strong tower against the foe.
>
> I long to dwell in your tent forever
>   and take refuge in the shelter of your wings.
> (Psalm 61:1–4)

I believe that Jesus held tightly to that rock while he was on earth, as he referred to this song of David while on the cross:

> Turn your ear to me,
>   come quickly to my rescue;
> be my rock of refuge,
>   a strong fortress to save me.
> Since you are my rock and my fortress,
>   for the sake of your name lead and guide me.
> Keep me free from the trap that is set for me,
>   for you are my refuge.
> Into your hands I commit my spirit;
>   deliver me, LORD, my faithful God. (Psalm 31:2–5)

Wisdom Clings to the Rock

FOR REFLECTION

Reflect on some of your most trying times. To whom did you first turn? To what did you turn? Consider ways that Jesus can become an increasingly solid rock for you as you go through life's challenges. What scriptures might help you remember that Jesus is the only solid rock? What songs help you to focus on the solid rock of Jesus? Spend some time reading these scriptures and reading or singing the lyrics to these songs.

Father, you are my rock. From the ends of the earth, I call to you, I call as my heart grows faint; lead me to you, the rock that is higher than I. You, God, are my refuge, my strong tower against the foes of life. I long to dwell in your tent forever and take refuge in the shelter of your wings. I need you, God, my solid rock. In Jesus' name, Amen.

30

WISDOM BUILDS FAITH
WHILE EXPRESSING LOVE

A couple of weeks after we were engaged to be married, Wyndham moved to North Carolina to serve in the campus ministry, while I finished my last quarter of college classes. (I would still do an internship in North Carolina.) We were both crazy busy during the five months of our engagement. He was in a new place starting a campus ministry, and I was taking a ridiculous number of credit hours to finish school, leading a Bible talk or two, and planning a wedding.

Long-distance calls were expensive back then, thus restrictive (given Wyndham's salary of seven thousand dollars a year, and my salary of nothing). We seldom were able to talk, but instead wrote letters during our five-month engagement. I wrote every day. Wyndham wrote some days—until my mentor, Ann Lucas, advised me to stop writing for a few days so he would understand what those letters meant. She was wise. He started writing every day.

Those letters meant so much to me that I still have them in a box in our basement. Years ago (perhaps it was

Wisdom Builds Faith While Expressing Love

our twenty-fifth anniversary), we read some of the letters together. They were filled with faith in what God would do and filled with awe at what he was doing in the campus ministry where Wyndham was working. The letters were filled with the conviction that nothing would be impossible for God. We believed the fields were ripe for harvest. This included students, professors, teens, and adults. We watched God move in people's lives as they became Christians. I heard about them in his letters. I felt his excitement, and I caught his vision. His attitude of faith conveyed in the letters could best be expressed by Paul's words in Ephesians 3:20–21:

> Now to him who is able to do immeasurably more than all we ask or imagine, according to his power that is at work within us, to him be glory in the church and in Christ Jesus throughout all generations, for ever and ever! Amen.

These letters also told me how much I was loved. I'd read those parts of the letters again and again. Wyndham's wisdom had (and has) the unique ability to build faith while expressing love. Wisdom does that—builds faith and expresses love. It's not a technique or writing style, but an overflow of faith and love from the heart.

God's letters to me, in his word, build faith and express love beyond any other letters. They leave me with faith and leave me feeling loved. This past week one of my assignments (I'm working on my master's degree in spiritual formation) included writing a letter to myself from God during the current season of my life. This was an emotionally moving exercise for me. My fingers typed faster than I can ever remember, and the whole time I was crying. Ugly crying.

145

Weeping. I felt God expressing his love for me (and for Wyndham) and reassuring me that he loves us, hears all our prayers, and is always aware of our situation. In this letter, he was telling me he "had this," and I could trust him. Here are a few excerpts.

My dear daughter,

As you enjoy another sunrise today and experience my reminders and kisses to you through your favorite autumn flowers, the crispness of the air, the wildlife that you enjoy, and the love you feel and experience in your heart...remember this is what I want for you. Trust me.

If only you could see as I do, you would understand that I would do nothing, ever, to hurt you. You know how deeply you feel about your children and grandchildren. Well, the love I feel for you is infinitely more. Trust that. You will see it one day. I will hold you in my arms, and as my Spirit lives in you now, I want you to feel hugged from the inside out. Trust me.

I hate that you are hurting and that your husband is suffering, but trust me. I feel this with you. I am suffering with you. This is temporary, and one day it will be a speck so small you will say... oh...now I get it. I will never leave you alone. I will be with you and him and your family every step of the way. I have this...

And that husband of yours... He is one of my dearest sons. Don't ever think I don't have him on and in my heart every day. Know beyond the shadow of a doubt I love you both. I can't wait to

Wisdom Builds Faith While Expressing Love

be together one day. Meanwhile, represent me well; don't ever quit giving. I'm going to lead you to many people who need help finding me. I will help you use the gifts I have given you. We are a team. You are my friend. Don't ever forget that, daughter.

I haven't forgotten your devotion to me. Never forget mine to you. Please take the time to be still and let this sink in. And always trust me. I've got this.

Always and forever yours,
Abba

As I reminisced about God's faithfulness to me and his words to me in the Scriptures (not just my imaginary letter), my faith was built. Wisdom builds faith while expressing love.

For Reflection

Take some time to be still and pray. Then, write a letter you think God might write to you in this season of your life.

Father, I stand amazed that you care to communicate with me, love me, and delight in me. Help me be continually aware of your presence, that I will reflect your love in all my emotions, attitudes, and conversations. I long to hear you as I read your word and be still long enough to hear your Spirit in my life. I love you my Abba, Father. Amen.

31

WISDOM BRINGS
ABIDING FRIENDSHIP

by Gary Dollar

[Love] always protects, always trusts, always hopes,
always perseveres. (1 Corinthians 13:7)

It was the fall of 1989, near what would likely have
been the end of my life, when I met Wyndham. My family
and I were stationed at Fort Devens in Ayer, Massachusetts. I had been a career soldier in the Army since 1975,
and over the previous fourteen years, I had become se-
verely addicted to alcohol. My attempts at sobriety had
been futile, including a treatment program at one of the
best inpatient centers in the country. I had become hopeless, emotionally hollow, and suicidal. Somehow, I was still
alive, but my internal organs ached. I was dying.

Even though I was reaping what I sowed and getting
what I deserved, my wife, Susan, my son, Aaron, and my
daughter, Andrea, were innocent and never should have
experienced the hell I introduced into their lives through:

- Physical and emotional abuse
- Fits of rage
- Infidelity
- Legal separations and constant threats of di-
  vorce

148

Wisdom Brings Abiding Friendship

- Broken promises to change, creating optimism followed by heartbreak
- Kids living fatherless for much of their adolescent lives
- Susan living husbandless, in fear and loneliness
- Hypocrisy – This "man" of the house was a respected and well-liked police officer during all the insanity, and consequently, they were forced to live the lie outside the home as a happy and healthy family.

Hurricane Florence struck the Carolinas with a vengeance in September 2018. It caused fifty-three deaths and over sixteen billion dollars in damages. It made landfall while bringing sustained winds of over 140 mph and overwhelming floods. Those who ignored the advice to get out but survived the onslaught were comforted when Florence passed over and continued on her way. They were oblivious to the devastation until they wandered outside. It would take years to rebuild—and even so, things will never be the same. My life had been like Hurricane Florence, causing great damage and devastation; however, thank God, rescuers came to help.

In the last half of 1989, Susan and I were introduced to Jesus and became disciples. (Apparently, nothing is impossible with God.) Repentance produced a time of refreshing for the entire family. My external changes were obvious. I stopped drinking and smoking as well as using "Army dialect," and Susan learned to find peace in God and gain trust in her heavenly Father to protect her. The storm that presented our most immediate threats had passed over, but it was the deep-rooted devastation to our hearts and minds that presented the biggest risk to our future physical and spiritual lives.

Eight weeks after our conversions we were deployed to Germany. Even though I told my new brothers that "I was all set," they insisted that Susan and I spend some time with the Shaws for some marriage discipling time before departing. That was the first time we met Wyndham. He was nothing like we expected. We anticipated a stodgy, unrelatable priestlike man who would let us talk for a while and send us on our way with some superficial advice; however, he was unpretentious and kind, and not only opened his home to us but also his heart—much like a loving father. We knew he was a "safe place." He was extremely compassionate and never gave a hint of condescension, arrogance, or superiority. That day Susan and I confessed sin, cried, and shared things from our past that we had kept secret for years. He was open with his life and masterfully handled the Scriptures, laying the biblical foundation for a godly marriage. I left his house that day knowing that I had a real friend. While I served in Germany, the Shaws always scheduled time with us during the European Missions Conference, in spite of the huge roles and responsibilities they had at those events. Each time we met, no matter how long the separation, they treated us like we had been together the day before and were always concerned with the progress of our marriage, asking Susan how things were going. I'm not sure why they didn't ask me...

Sadly, over the years, there have been times when I allowed my past life to resurface. These were some of my

Wisdom Brings Abiding Friendship

darkest moments that at times caused me in shame to turn my back on God, in some cases for a long time. Wyndham frequently reached out to me and let me know he was praying for me. And the few times when the situation became desperate, in love, he fearlessly came to my side to encourage and call me back to God. It was those times that led me to repentance and back to the church family.

> From one man he made all the nations, that they should inhabit the whole earth; and he marked out their appointed times in history and the boundaries of their lands. God did this so that they would seek him and perhaps reach out for him and find him, though he is not far from any one of us.
> (Acts 17:26–27)

God, in his providence, brought us back to Fort Devens from Germany. I have since retired from the army, moved with my family to a neighboring town near the Shaws, gained further education, entered the civilian workforce, and recently retired. Wyndham and I became the best of friends through all these times. No man has done more to save my marriage, my life, and ultimately my soul. His carrying of me through the hard times has created a bond between us that will last into eternity. I am so thankful to God that he determined for me this appointed time in history at this exact place.

> There are friends who pretend to be friends, but there is a friend who sticks closer than a brother. (Proverbs 18:24 RSV)

FOR REFLECTION

If you have wandered from God with secret (or not so secret) sin, determine to talk to God and to whomever can help you find your way back. If you have a strong relationship with God, determine to be more alert to those who are hurting and need help finding God again. Pray to have the heart of compassion that never gives up on your friends.

Father, thank you that you have put me in a spiritual family. Thank you that you not only empower me to change, but you also put other disciples in my life to help me be transformed into your likeness. Help me be humble, always willing to let others into my life. Help me be compassionate and selfless, persistently caring about my brothers and sisters in Christ. Thank you that you never give up on me. Help me to be like you. In Jesus' name, Amen.

32

WISDOM SPEAKS
WITH THE END IN MIND

Words are funny things. They are powerful. God created the world through the power in his words. Words play many roles in our lives. What do they do? Inspire. Instruct. Hurt. Convict. Comfort. Entertain. Enlighten. As they do their jobs, they produce varied emotions in the speaker and the hearer. When we hear words we may cry, laugh, sigh, smile, cringe, or even scream.

Have you ever longed to own a "word catcher" that could catch careless words somewhere between your mouth and someone's ear? I have. Unfortunately, there is no such thing—so the burden is on the speaker. If not careful, as the Red Sox slogan would read, "Damage done."

Wyndham asked me a wise and rather profound question this week. I was in conversation with someone who was assisting us in a particular caretaking task. Everything was good. Perceiving a problem, I communicated something to this person in the form of a question, reminder, and plea. I didn't raise my voice, and I tried to be kind and positive. However, this was not the first time I had spoken similar words to this person, and the words have yet to be well received. As I think back, maybe this was the fifth or sixth time over the past year I have spoken similar words. I thought perhaps the time was right to bring up the previously visited topic. Again.

Well, it wasn't.

After the person didn't react well, the mood changed. Wyndham asked me later, "So, what were you hoping to accomplish?"

I thought about this question for a while. *What was I trying to accomplish?* I did feel, upon evaluation, that I was trying to bring about needed change for that person's (and my) well-being. However, I thought through other times I've had this same conversation. What did I seek to accomplish then? Some of those answers would have been to let the person know: *I don't approve. I want you to know my level of frustration. You're not doing "it" the right way.*

Whenever words are born of frustration, or dare I say condemnation, they don't accomplish good. They don't strengthen relationships. While the end we hope to accomplish may be right, timing and attitude are key. It is wise to ask: *How will my words affect the relationship? What am I hoping to accomplish? How would I feel if I put myself in the hearer's place? Am I most concerned about speaking my words, or am I more concerned about the overall welfare of the hearer?*

I would wish Paul to describe me as he does Timothy in Philippians 2:19–20:

> I hope in the Lord Jesus to send Timothy to you soon, that I also may be cheered when I receive news about you. I have no one else like him, who will show genuine concern for your welfare.

Wisdom Speaks with the End in Mind

I must get "me" out of the equation and wait until the emotions of the moment pass and frustration levels wane. While speaking the truth in love is needed and right (Ephesians 4:15), wisdom is needed for when and how to speak the truth. Often, this can be determined by stopping to consider the wise question:

What am I hoping to accomplish?

FOR REFLECTION

Think through a recent conversation you have had that did not go well. Perhaps you did all you could do, but perhaps there was more that you could have considered. Ask yourself: *What was I hoping to accomplish?* Pray to have the good of the other person in mind in all your conversations.

Holy Father, forgive me when I don't consider the words I let escape from my mouth. Please give me the heart of Timothy, who had a genuine concern for others' welfare. Help me to get my selfish emotions out of the way so that I might speak and convey the deepest love, even when I need to say something difficult. Please keep me from frustration and condemnation, enabling me to speak with patience and hope. In Jesus' name, Amen.

33

WISDOM LIVES TODAY

I'm often asked, "How are you doing?" This is a loaded question. I appreciate the question, yet I don't know how to respond without prefacing my answer with "today." Today I am doing okay. Today is the only day I know I have on this earth, though I am confident I have endless spiritual "todays." With the progression of Wyndham's illness, we treasure today—each day. Each new day is a gift and because it is precious, I think of today a bit differently than I used to. Things that once seemed important often don't carry the value they once did. I know things may get even more difficult physically for him, and for me, but we choose not to focus on this. Anticipatory fatigue, anticipatory anxiety, and anticipatory grief are real things.

Things we don't wish to choose. Thus, we focus on today.

Today I can do the most important things. I can love God and love people. I can be loved by God and be loved by others. Today I can serve, and today I can live out God's purpose for my life. Today I can strive to help Wyndham have the best "today" possible. With God, and only with God, I can do today. And tomorrow, I can say the same thing. Living today keeps me focused on what I can be for

Wisdom Lives Today

God and others now, and it helps rid my mind of worry and regret. I now better understand Jesus' admonition to ask for daily bread. Today my faith must be real. I must live fully today. I know that many tomorrows will hold various difficult situations, because Jesus says, "In this world, you will have trouble." However, he continues with "I have overcome the world," so that we can have peace and take heart (John 16:33). Thankfully, this world is not my true home. God planned for us the life intended before the Fall (when sin entered). As I mention in my book *An Aging Grace*, his lovingkindness and grace kept us from the Tree of Life so we won't have to stay in a broken world forever. He has something amazing planned. However, to get there I must live well today.

When Wyndham was diagnosed with multiple system atrophy, his neurologist looked at us lovingly and said, "You will have the privilege to focus on the things that are most important. You will learn to live the way all of us should live every day." I could write a whole chapter on Dr. Khurana and what I've learned from him, but I'll limit this to a few sentences. He has a rare combination of gifts such as listening intently, showing compassion, focusing on the positive, knowing what to say and what not to say, eagerly wanting to help (giving his cell phone number and answering quickly), all while building you up. To add to this he is brilliant, yet humble. He is currently building brains from stem cells (in the Khurana Lab at Harvard... yes, it's named after him) in order to search for cures for this terrible disease. His team of researchers is making exciting progress as they seek to match antibodies with wayward proteins, hoping the antibodies will kill the proteins that fold improperly into the cells, thus wreaking havoc on the nervous system. I know this is a tangent, but Wyndham's neurologist understands the physical value of focusing on today, even while his research is for tomorrow.

Such is wise living. Wisdom understands that focusing (spiritually) on today is what prepares us for tomorrow. My faith must be strong today to prepare for the unknown tomorrow. How I live today affects how I spend eternity. I must wake up today with a pure focus on loving God and loving people, and being loved by God and by people. Certainly, I get distracted and fall short, but this is my goal each day. The scriptures below (and many more) instruct me on today (emphasis added):

> This is the day that the LORD has made;
>   let us rejoice and be glad in it.
> (Psalm 118:24 NRSV)

> For he is our God,
>   and we are the people of his pasture,
>   and the sheep of his hand.
>
> O that today you would listen to his voice!
> (Psalm 95:7 NRSV)

> "Give us today our daily bread."
> (Matthew 6:11 NIV)

> "So don't worry about tomorrow, for tomorrow will bring its own worries. Today's trouble is enough for today." (Matthew 6:34 NLT)

> The lines of purpose in your lives never grow slack, tightly tied as they are to your future in heaven, kept taut by hope. The Message is as true among you today as when you first heard it. It doesn't diminish or weaken over time. (Colossians 1:5 MSG)

Wisdom Lives Today

So watch your step, friends. Make sure there's no evil unbelief lying around that will trip you up and throw you off course, diverting you from the living God. For as long as it's still God's *Today*, keep each other on your toes so sin doesn't slow down your reflexes. If we can only keep our grip on the sure thing we started out with, we're in this with Christ for the long haul.

These words keep ringing in our ears:

Today, please listen;
don't turn a deaf ear as in the bitter uprising.
(Hebrews 3:12–15 MSG)

Since everything here *today* might well be gone tomorrow, do you see how essential it is to live a holy life? Daily expect the Day of God, eager for its arrival. The galaxies will burn up and the elements melt down that day—but we'll hardly notice. We'll be looking the other way, ready for the promised new heavens and the promised new earth, all landscaped with righteousness.

So, my dear friends, since this is what you have to look forward to, do your very best to be found living at your best, in purity and peace.
(2 Peter 3:11–14 MSG)

So, I ask—how are you today?

FOR REFLECTION

Consider ways you worry about what is to come. How does this affect you? At the end of your day today, reflect on what you thought about and what you did. Do your thoughts and actions reflect what is most important? If not, what is one thing you can do to change this?

Father, you have said our times are in your hands. Let me live fully for today, not worrying about tomorrow or fretting about yesterday. Help my choices in spending time, the words I speak, and the thoughts that fill my mind reflect on what is most important. Father, give me today my daily bread. Not too much that I might become self-sufficient or ungrateful, or too little that I might be tempted to worry. Please help me to live today well, pleasing to you. In Jesus' name, Amen.

34

WISDOM FINDS
THE END OF ME

The Christmas festivities were over. The tree lights were turned off, and a blissful, satisfying feeling of exhaustion set in as my head hit the pillow. The bliss and satisfaction were soon awakened and diverted by approximately five hundred sneezes and a feeling of cement in my head. As I got up to get tissues, I quickly realized that my knee felt injured, shooting excruciating pain at every turn and with every step. Over the week, the illness subsided but the knee pain has not (MRI coming soon). At first, it was annoying, but as it now affects my ability to help Wyndham without facing debilitating pain, it has at times felt unbearable. Several nights ago, the pain wouldn't stop. While I wish I could share that I felt complete trust and assurance that God was faithfully listening and working on our behalf, to be honest, my thoughts went more like this:

God, aren't we dealing with hard enough stuff already? Now this. Really? Are you trying to crush us? I've got nothing, God. Really, nothing. I feel utterly and completely helpless.

That sad mess was my "prayer."

I wasn't sure if my pillow was wet from the tears, or from the newly acquired conjunctivitis. (I don't share this stuff to garner sympathy [prayers are always appreciated, though], but rather to share raw and real thoughts...and how God entered the picture.)

Normally, I like and strive to live life with a "glass-half-full" perspective instead of a "glass-half-empty" point of view. Most often, I rely on God's love, count on hope, and feel deeply thankful. However, during this time my glass was not half full. It was not even half empty. It was dry as a bone—completely empty.

My emotions weren't pretty, but that's when God showed up in full force. Oh, he had been there, it's just that I couldn't fully feel his presence until I was utterly depleted... *I've got nothing. I'm completely helpless.* As I leaned into the suffering and cried out to God, I found I was soon leaning on Jesus. He had appeared in the suffering—as in an epiphany. Seldom, if ever, have I experienced this level of depth concerning the ways God uses suffering to bring me into his presence. A deep presence.

His presence is a relationship that fills our soul—one that experiences God. One that convinces us of what is truly important—the only thing that matters. A presence that tells us eternity has already started. One that inspires. One that convicts. One that takes us to our knees before him. His presence became deeper, and I'm grateful. As C.S. Lewis writes, "We can ignore even pleasure. But pain insists upon being attended to. God whispers to us in our pleasures, speaks in our conscience, but shouts in our pains."[3]

---

3. C.S. Lewis, *The Problem of Pain* (New York: Harper Collins, 1996), 81.

Wisdom Finds the End of Me

Suffering empties us, carrying us to the broken place where God can fill us. While I hate the pain of watching Wyndham's body deteriorate with his disease, I marvel at ways God is working (often unbeknownst to us) through this suffering. I don't know the answers as to why this has happened, but I observe that God empties us so that we can be more fully filled, so that we can truly see him in his magnificent glory. There is nothing more filling, or fulfilling, than experiencing our intimate relationship with God.

There are many ways I can think of that we could be more useful to God without the suffering, as our situation keeps us from many possibilities. Wyndham exhibits wisdom as he trusts that God completes the end of him. God is enough. I long to carry this wisdom with me, so that Christ may shine more brightly through me.

As I lay on my bed and wept, feeling depleted and useless, I was reminded by Paul that wisdom finds the end of me...so that God can take it from there. Once we get to the end of ourselves, we can more clearly see and feel him.

> We are pressed on every side by troubles, but we are not crushed. We are perplexed, but not driven to despair. We are hunted down, but never abandoned by God. We get knocked down, but we are not destroyed. Through suffering, our bodies continue to share in the death of Jesus so that the life of Jesus may also be seen in our bodies. (2 Corinthians 4:8–10 NLT)

May we all see him clearer, as we find the end of ourselves and watch God take over. It is through our weaknesses that somehow, God makes us strong.

Three times I pleaded with the Lord to take [the thorn in my flesh] away from me.

But he said to me, "My grace is sufficient for you, for my power is made perfect in weakness." Therefore I will boast all the more gladly about my weaknesses, so that Christ's power may rest on me. That is why, for Christ's sake, I delight in weaknesses, in insults, in hardships, in persecutions, in difficulties. For when I am weak, then I am strong.

(2 Corinthians 12:8–10)

For Reflection

Read 2 Corinthians 12:8–10 out loud several times. Consider what this scripture means to you and how the Lord's grace can be sufficient for you. Meditate on this scripture throughout the day. Consider what your life would look like if your weaknesses became strengths. God can do this. Pray that you can truly believe this scripture.

Glorious Father, in my struggles, help me trust. The challenges in my life don't feel good. Help me to delight in my weaknesses, knowing your power works mightily in them. Let your grace be enough for me, Father. I ask that you give me the Spirit of wisdom and revelation, that I may know you better. Open the eyes of my heart to know the hope to which you have called me. Let me understand the riches of your glorious inheritance. Mighty God, I know when I better understand that the power in me is the same power that raised Jesus from the dead I will step out with radical faith. You alone, God, have all power, glory, and love. In awe of you I pray, Amen.

35

WISDOM OVERLOOKS

Recently, a difficult situation resulted in hurt feelings. Mine. To me, "fairness" has always been important. When I feel inequity, mine or someone else's, I can struggle to pull my thoughts back to Jesus. Jesus was a victim extraordinaire of unthinkable inequity—yet he entrusted himself to the one who judges justly. While I was wrestling with these fairness thoughts I "happened upon" an article seemingly written just for me—at just the right time. It was from Vaneetha Rendall Risner's blog, *Dancing in the Rain*, concerning the word "overlook." Her words (emphasis mine) caught my attention:

> I remembered a speaker who said *the best way to love people is to remember them as their best selves. That means not dwelling on the things they've done wrong but rather focusing on what they've done right.* Rehearsing their strengths rather than their faults. Remembering the times they have shown up for me and the times they have been kind and thoughtful rather than when they've wounded me. *In short, one way to love people is to overlook their offenses.*

Many scriptures teach this wisdom. Here are three:

A person's wisdom yields patience;
   it is to one's glory to overlook an offense.
(Proverbs 19:11)

165

> Fools show their annoyance at once,
> but the prudent overlook an insult.
> (Proverbs 12:16)

> Overlook an offense and bond a friendship;
> fasten on to a slight and—good-bye, friend!
> (Proverbs 17:9 MSG)

So much truth radiates from these verses. Yes, offenses are real. These verses acknowledge this. Yes, we are to be honest and seek resolution with our offenders in the ways the Bible teaches. No, it is not loving to be an enabler. However, it is easy to be annoyed by offenses that in the big picture of life are inconsequential—like the past week when a server at a fast-food drive-through gave me the wrong meal four times, none even resembling our order...or when someone visiting the park across the street parked in front of my mailbox so that my mail was not delivered, or when I stood in a checkout line while the person in front of me appeared to be finished but then pulled out unsorted coupons and for fifteen minutes cut coupons...after which his card was declined three times. (Yes, I did try to pay the cashier for his order, but he refused...and I confess, I'm not sure if my offer was fully out of benevolence or out of frustration.) Or when someone promised to do something I was counting on and then didn't. You get the point. I won't mention more, or my blood pressure may rise. See what I mean? Just. Let. Go.

Wyndham excels in the ability to "overlook." At times, to be honest, his ability to overlook has annoyed me when I didn't want him to overlook something. But he is right. He somehow sees right through weaknesses and mistakes to the best of who that person is and what that person can be. I strive to imitate this, but I confess it's hard.

Wisdom Overlooks

Vaneetha, in her blog, shared a well-known story of two monks:

> Two monks were walking together when they came across a wealthy young woman who was trying to cross a large mud puddle. The older monk picked up the woman and carried her across the puddle, placing her safely on the other side. The woman said not a word of thanks.
>
> The monks walked back to the monastery in silence, but hours later, as they neared their destination, the younger one said to the older, "I still can't believe she didn't thank you. That woman was so ungrateful."
>
> The older monk responded, "I put her down hours ago. Why are you still carrying her?"

Good question, right?

Wisdom overlooks.

And wisdom is willing to be overlooked.

God is an overlooker in various ways.

I'm grateful that as God "overlooks" his creation—while sin is serious and does not go unpunished (read Hebrews 10:29 in the Message version), his grace, given through Jesus, overlooks the offenses of all who are in Christ.

Instead of seeing the sin, he sees the love and service of those who follow Jesus. I'm eternally grateful that God, through Jesus, overlooks my sin—yet amazingly doesn't overlook my heart or service. Wow.

> For God is not unjust; he will not overlook your work and the love that you showed for his sake in serving the saints, as you still do.
> (Hebrews 6:10 NRSV)

As I think about ways wisdom "overlooks," I envision stopping at our favorite overlook to view the rocky coast where the sea often glitters like diamonds. (We once saw a whale in this spot.) However, as I step outside preparing to enjoy God's majesty, I miss the whole beautiful scene because I become focused on a bag of litter that someone threw on the ground. I then become indignant about the thoughtlessness of the litterer as I "valiantly" clean up what they left behind. What a sad scene this becomes.

Overlook the litter,
To behold the beauty

What a shame to focus on the litter and miss the glitter.

Wisdom overlooks. Will we?

For Reflection

Think of things that annoy you, and ask yourself how big these things are in the big picture of life. Consider how you might more quickly overlook at least one of these things. Memorize one of the above proverbs about overlooking so that when you feel annoyed you can bring this verse to your mind and practice becoming thankful for something that person does, or a situation in which you find yourself.

> *Gracious Father, how I must annoy you at times. Thank you for overlooking my sin through Jesus and teaching me to become more like you. I wish to please you, not annoy you. Help me learn to be one who brings you joy.*

Wisdom Overlooks

I pray that I can be quick to overlook offenses and become a more gracious person. How greatly I depend on your grace and mercy. In Jesus' name, Amen.

36

WISDOM KNOWS "BUSY'S" PURPOSE

It's an oft-spoken phrase: *I'm so busy!* Life seems to fly by at rocket speed. Even when not busy working, we are busy checking phones, working remotes, and dashing kids to and from activities. "Busy" can be necessary, but it can also become a trap. A habit. A competition. A source of our sense of worth or security. It is of utmost importance to discern the reason behind our busy. Ultimately, is it to help bring glory to God?

> The wisdom of the prudent is to give thought to
> their ways,
> but the folly of fools is deception.
> (Proverbs 14:8)

Wyndham often spoke of a reply I told him that my dad used to give when someone asked him his occupation. I can still hear how my dad would answer while wearing a big smile on his face: "My occupation is dean of admissions at the University of Florida, but my preoccupation is the Kingdom of God." There was no doubt in my mind what was of first importance in my dad's life and our family's life.

Wyndham has lived a busy life, but now he lives life at a slow pace. No deadlines. No phone calls. No emails or

Wisdom Knows "Busy's" Purpose

texts. No travels. No traffic. He is able to focus on what is truly important. Important has taken on new meanings. What often seemed urgent has since lost importance. What is truly important has become what is more urgent. For Wyndham, his disease numbers his days—that is, without divine intervention. Truthfully, we all need to live with our earthly purpose and heaven in mind—because we all have numbered days.

> So teach us to number our days
>   that we may get a heart of wisdom.
> (Psalm 90:12 RSV)

One nugget of Wyndham's wisdom that stands out to me and that I try to emulate is his response toward busyness. He was always busy, but never too busy to love God first and then love people. He was never too busy to be deeply involved and connected to me and our children. He was never too busy for people. He decided to live this way.

When we are busy, people can feel hesitant to approach us. When Wyndham was approached, people often said something like: *I'd love to get some time with you or get some advice from you, but I know you are so busy.* Wyndham would stop, reach out a reassuring arm, look them in the eyes and say, "You *are my busy.*" By that, he meant that people were his priority. He was never too busy for people—to love them and to serve them. Who is our busy for? What will our busy mean a hundred years from now? Money won't matter. Sports won't matter. Our degrees won't matter. Our looks won't matter.

Our relationship with God will matter.

We have often advised others: *If you are too busy to keep spiritual priorities and build meaningful relationships, then you are just too busy. Something must change.* We can even be busy doing spiritual activities while missing the heart of God and people. If we do "busy" without the heart of Jesus, we will be exhausted and ineffective.

Tonight, as I participated in my online class collaborative session, I asked my professor a question. As part of his response, he emailed me the following quote from John Piper's *The Pleasures of God: Meditations on God's Delight in Being God.* It reminded me that "busy" flows well from the soul filled by God.

> God has no needs that I could ever be required to satisfy. God has no deficiencies that I might be required to supply. He is complete in himself. He is overflowing with happiness in the fellowship of the Trinity. The upshot of this is that God is a mountain spring, not a watering trough. A mountain spring is self-replenishing. It constantly overflows and supplies others. But a watering trough needs to be filled with a pump or bucket brigade. So if you want to glorify the worth of a spring you do it by getting down on your hands and knees and drinking to your heart's satisfaction, until you have the refreshment and strength to go back down into the valley and tell people what you've found. You do not glorify a mountain spring by dutifully hauling water up to the path from

Wisdom Knows "Busy's" Purpose

the river below and dumping it in the spring...the way to please God is to come to him to get and not to give, to drink and not to water. He is most glorified in us when we are most satisfied in him... God is the kind of God who will be pleased with the one thing I have to offer—my thirst.

As a popular commercial implores, "Remain thirsty, my friends." Then, we will be energized for purposeful "busy."

FOR REFLECTION

Take some extended time to be still with God. Reflect on the pace of your life to determine whether God is at the center of your activities or if busyness takes center stage. Make some decisions that allow God to take priority, not only in actions but in thought and friendship.

My Father who is beyond time, you are worthy of all honor and priority. Help me to be still before you in order to experience your love. I repent of all idols in my life, even when they take the form of "good things." May I never be too busy for you or to see others as you see them. I know I don't have to earn your love through my performance, so help me to live my life with first-love for you and a devotion to you that follows that love. In Jesus' name, Amen.

37

WISDOM CONSIDERS

Every once in a while, a kind note or message arrives as a pleasant surprise—like when you hear from someone you haven't seen or spoken with for decades. I have been learning the value of kind words, and words that express appreciation. Kind words mean a great deal. Many of you have expressed such kindness that Wyndham and I are eternally grateful for you.

As I write these chapters, I have several goals in mind. One is to honor a man I love and respect deeply. Another is to share wisdom observed from his life, in hopes that it can spark practical spiritual growth, encouragement, or inspiration.

Another purpose of this book is personal. Writing helps me to recount precious memories and things I have learned (and am learning) as I process what the aggressive and progressive nature of Wyndham's illness brings. It brings me a deep current and anticipatory grief (and sometimes fear), yet somehow this is accompanied by inexpressible gratitude, intimacy with God, trust, and a peace that passes human understanding. (Thank you, God.)

This chapter's nugget of Wyndham's wisdom, from an old friend we have not seen for many decades, recounts yet another important quality of wisdom—consideration. All too often, it's easy to keep conversations shallow and incomplete, leaving relationships at a standstill. The Scriptures

Wisdom Considers

teach us to consider how to stir each other up to love and good deeds.

> And let us consider how we may spur one another on toward love and good deeds.
>
> (Hebrews 10:24)

"Consider" means we think through, study, and meditate on something. Wyndham excels at learning (considering) and valuing people—often resulting in stirrings of love and kindness. Today Jerry Sprague, an "old" friend from our campus ministry days in Raleigh, North Carolina, sent the following note:

> Wyndham was very instrumental in my spiritual growth when I was a young Christian. I grew up not knowing how to communicate negative feelings, so I would always stuff them inside. One time, Wyndham and I were supposed to meet somewhere, and he forgot. When he realized it, he approached me in fellowship and apologized. I gave him my typical response, "Oh, that's okay; no big deal." He looked me straight in the eyes and said, **Brother, tell me how you really feel. That's the only way I can ever get to know you.**

That moment had a tremendous impact on my spiritual development. I should have verbalized how disappointed I was and that it did hurt me; in scriptural terms, "speaking the truth in love." That's the first time I really understood what it meant to be open and to speak the truth in love. God used Wyndham to teach me this truth.

It was still a struggle to be that open, but that was the starting point! Wyndham was always so gentle with me, and we continued to have a warm and effective relationship. I remember shedding tears when he told me he was moving. He had been such an inspiration to me. Please give him my love and thank him for the love he showed me!

May we all use *consideration* in our conversations. We never know the effect our words can have.

For Reflection

Think about the next conversation you know you will have with someone. Considering Hebrews 10:24 and Jerry's message, think of a way your thought and prayer before this conversation can make it more meaningful, encouraging, and pleasing to God.

Father, thank you for considering me. Help me to be thoughtful and to take time to consider how to make every conversation upbuilding, gracious, and seasoned with salt. May the words of my mouth and the meditations of my heart be pleasing and acceptable to you, my God. In Jesus' name, Amen

38

WISDOM
Throws a Pebble

Though we had to tromp through the snow to get to the creek beside our house, I decided today would be a good day to introduce our youngest grandchild to the thrill of throwing pebbles off the bridge into the water. Through the years, all our grandchildren have enjoyed this little adventure. This afternoon little Colette held two pebbles in her tiny hand, I held one in my wrinkling hand—and on the count of three, we heaved them off the bridge and into the water, with a splat and a plunk.

As the pebbles dropped to the bottom and out of sight, we could only see the ripples that they produced. Where those ripples traveled, I have no idea. The little creek next to our house ebbs and flows, sometimes swiftly and sometimes barely moving, and eventually meets a river (I think the Ipswich), which flows into the Atlantic. As we watched the ripples fade out of sight I thought of a scripture from the book on wisdom, Ecclesiastes 11:1, 5–6:

> Cast your bread upon the waters,
> for after many days you will find it again…

As you do not know the path of the wind,
    or how the body is formed in a mother's womb,
so you cannot understand the work of God,
    the Maker of all things.

Sow your seed in the morning,
    and at evening let not your hands be idle,
for you do not know which will succeed,
    whether this or that,
    or whether both will do equally well. (NIV1984)

Colette (Coco) is a tiny, precious little two-year-old, and I'm a not-so-tiny 65-year-old. There was nothing strong or eventful about our throws, and our pebbles were small. But we threw them—and the ripples began. Like the small pebbles, we never know where our seemingly small actions will take the ensuing ripples as we strive to follow Jesus— through good deeds, prayer, words of encouragement, sharing our testimony, and sharing the Scriptures. The energy of the Spirit of God carries the ripples from our meager pebbles in ways and to places we cannot imagine.

This week I received an email from Don Lee, a dear friend we met while in our twenties and leading a campus ministry in Raleigh, North Carolina. We certainly lacked experience and expertise, but we had a whole lot of faith in our great God. Don was a student at Duke University who became a Christian during this time. Every year without fail, for the past forty-two years, he has called Wyndham on the anniversary of his baptism into Christ to thank him for sharing Jesus with him—for "throwing that pebble." He gave me permission to share his note:

> *Wyndham, I've been mulling over for several days how to express my gratitude to you for studying the*

Wisdom Throws a Pebble

Bible with me 43 years ago. I'll never forget that time. I was a shy, unconfident, fearful, and empty young man in my freshman year at Duke University. My sister Nancy "set me up" to meet you and study the Bible. Each week I'd make the drive from Durham to Raleigh and meet you at the Brooks Avenue Church of Christ. Your piercing eyes would see right through me. I felt exposed but at the same time accepted by you. Your patience in walking each step of my new spiritual journey with me was essential.

At one point I said, "Let's get me baptized." Instead of being fired up about my decision, you dug deeper to make sure I had dealt with some issues with my family being lord of my life before Jesus. I'm so thankful you risked our relationship to help me get over this obstacle. There's no way I could have persevered for this long without being tested early on. Since the time you studied with me so many years ago, I've only gotten to follow you from afar. All that you've shared (as well as so many others' contributions) makes me wish that I could have been around you more!

One of Jeanie's musings about "overlooking" helped me so much. As many will testify, your legacy and impact reach far and wide. While most of the ministries you have been in are on the East Coast (FL, NC, WV, MA), few people realize the worldwide impact. That small North Carolina campus ministry included Douglas Arthur (London), Douglas Jacoby (global teacher), and Gary Knutson (Johannesburg). Your legacy has reached to China as well. Other disciples from that ministry (Scott and Lynne Green and I) went to China. God used the Greens to plant the Hong Kong church in 1997. There are now 27 churches with almost 4000 disciples in the China region. What more can I say? I think of you and Jeanie often. Your faith and courage to finish the fight inspire me. I love you. Thank you for sharing God's word with me. Love, your Brother in Christ, Don

God's word is powerful. We just have to throw the pebbles. The Spirit of God will take the ripples from there—in mysterious and unimaginable ways.

> "For my thoughts are not your thoughts,
>   neither are your ways my ways,"
>   declares the Lord.
> "As the heavens are higher than the earth,
>   so are my ways higher than your ways
>   and my thoughts than your thoughts.
> As the rain and the snow
>   come down from heaven,
> and do not return to it
>   without watering the earth
> and making it bud and flourish,
>   so that it yields seed for the sower and bread for
>   the eater,
> so is my word that goes out from my mouth:
>   It will not return to me empty,
> but will accomplish what I desire
>   and achieve the purpose for which I sent it."
> (Isaiah 55:8–11)

Throw that pebble today, and by faith...wait for God to do more than you dare ask or imagine.

Wisdom Throws a Pebble

FOR REFLECTION

What proverbial pebble can you throw today? Pray that God will take your words and deeds and multiply them for his purposes. As you share your faith, speak encouraging words to someone, or show compassion, know that God can do amazing things with our meager actions and words.

Loving Father, please take my words and actions and use them for your purposes and to your glory. Help me be alert to opportunities to do good, to share my faith, and to bring encouragement to others. I know you will multiply my efforts, but help me be consistent in throwing the pebbles. May I always focus on your love and power and on others' needs before my own. I rely on your Spirit to do this; I cannot do it on my own. I need you every moment of every day. Amen.

39

WISDOM TREASURES TIME

Time—how do you view it?

When I was a child, I measured time by Christmases. The span from one year to the next felt eternal. Now, I at times wonder why I should even bother to take down the tree. It seems a blink before it's time to put it up again. Has it already been three months since Christmas?

It seems such a short time ago when our first grandchild was born. So how is it that she just drove over here to visit her papa tonight?

This year I turned sixty-five and joined the world of Medicare. How can this be? As my friend Gordon once bemoaned, "Time is funny. At first, it goes slowly, but once you hit sixty it's a freefall. " Truth.

Time is precious. Each one of these grains of sand in this hourglass is valuable, not to be wasted or taken for granted. Each grain should represent a day lived to the full, according to God's purposes.

I often wonder how God views time—since it is measured for us, but not for him. Really, what are two seconds or a hundred years compared to eternity? If I could understand God's thinking, or fathom how he viewed such

Wisdom Treasures Time

things, then I suppose he would not be God. His under-standing is in another dimension altogether. And honestly, that's comforting for me. Whether it may be the days of cre-ation, or a day when the sun stood still—God does not measure time as we do. He is timeless.

We are all given a portion of measured time here on earth, yet we never know how many grains of sand are in our hourglass. Wyndham's illness has driven this point home for me. I envisioned these years to be full of living out dreams together for God—yet the dreams are not as I pictured. And oh-so-much harder. While none of us know our times, the visible grains of sand in some hourglasses are fewer than in others.

I believe if I could but for a moment see time through God's eyes I would only fall down and worship—because his plans are perfect. I just can't see them in this physical dimension. God does not forget us. He is not deaf to our prayers. He is not blind to what is going on. He hears our sobs and is attentive to our pleas. Even our sighs are not lost on him. (And he heard a lot of those this week.) Thus I know there is something more going on than I can now know or understand.

Last weekend (in March 2019) we thought we had lost Wyndham. Friday night he seemed fine, with a little sore throat. I was not concerned, as Jacob stayed here while I went to my women's brunch Saturday morning. I came back home to find Wyndham burning to the touch, unre-sponsive, and with labored breathing. He could not com-municate, and breathing was difficult. Oxygen was low. The rest of the day all seventeen of us surrounded him with love, prayers, songs, and many tears. Sunday was not much different and Monday morning breathing was so difficult that he initiated our tearful goodbyes (or rather, "see you laters"), him wanting me to reassure him I would be okay. I can't describe the intense sorrow I felt, combined with hope, knowing I truly would see him later. He would now be the "lucky" one.

The timing was such that earlier that week we had decided to use a hospice team, though I wasn't sure it was needed. As God's providence would have it, the very first visit for signing the papers with a nurse occurred as I arrived home Saturday morning when he was in such decline. Within hours we had oxygen, a hospital bed, and a nurse for Saturday and Sunday. They did our thinking and procuring of things we didn't even know we needed or have any idea how to get. On Monday we met his official (wonderful) nurse, who came and saw him in this tough state— on oxygen, with a high fever, and unable to talk. Thinking it might be an infection, she contacted his doctor asking to put him on an antibiotic immediately. Over the next few days, his progress has been steady. Yesterday, when she arrived, he was in his wheelchair, smiling. (And I thought he might never sit in his chair again.) We knew, and she confirmed, that had he not responded to the penicillin he would not be here today. God gave us more time, for which I'm incredibly, deeply thankful...but it's not an easy time. Wyndham is weak, and life is hard. We know he will not always pull out of such a downturn, perhaps even the next time. But I'm grateful to have him longer. There are still more grains of sand in his hourglass.

Wyndham has always treasured the verse in Acts 13:36 and trusted in its message:

Wisdom Treasures Time

Now when David had served God's purpose in
his own generation, he fell asleep (Acts 13:36a).

We trust that God allows us to serve his purpose in our
generation, and whatever unseen aims this may involve, it
always involves trust.

One of my favorite (but hard) scriptures is in Psalm 31:

Since you are my rock and my fortress,
for the sake of your name lead and guide me.
Keep me free from the trap that is set for me,
for you are my refuge.
Into your hands I commit my spirit;
deliver me, LORD, my faithful God...
Be merciful to me, LORD, for I am in distress;
my eyes grow weak with sorrow,
my soul and body with grief...
My times are in your hands;
deliver me from the hands of my enemies,
from those who pursue me.
Let your face shine on your servant;
save me in your unfailing love...
Be strong and take heart,
all you who hope in the LORD.
(Psalm 31:3–5, 9, 15–16, 24 (emphasis added)

Our times *are* in his hands. His hands are big enough,
strong enough, and tender enough. He doesn't accidentally
drop the hourglass and say, *Whoops. Didn't mean that.* Our
times are in his steady, mighty, *never-failing* hands.

Treasure the time you have today. Live in a way that
will truly matter a hundred years from now, long after your
sands have emptied.

WEDNESDAYS WITH WYNDHAM

The following powerful words are excerpts from a sermon on Psalm 31 by Charles Spurgeon on May 17, 1881:

We are not in our own hands, nor in the hands of earthly teachers; but we are under the skillful operation of hands which make nothing in vain. The close of life is not decided by the sharp knife of the fates; but by the hand of love. We shall not die before our time, neither shall we be forgotten and left upon the stage too long.

Not only are we ourselves in the hand of the Lord, but all that surrounds us. Our times make up a kind of atmosphere of existence; and all this is under divine arrangement. We dwell within the palm of God's hand. We are absolutely at his disposal, and all our circumstances are arranged by him in all their details. We are comforted to have it so.

What a blessing it is to see by the eye of faith all things that concern you grasped in the hand of God! What peace as to every matter which could cause anxiety flows into the soul when we see all our hopes built upon so stable a foundation, and preserved by such supreme power! "My times are in thy hand!"

FOR REFLECTION

Consider if you knew that you had thirty days left in your hourglass. How would you spend them? How would you set your priorities? What do you think God would say to you? Use these thoughts to help you put the important things in life over the urgent. What is one change you can make today?

Father, thank you that you are timeless. I don't understand that, as it is beyond my understanding. In the

186

Wisdom Treasures Time

days you give me, help me to put the most important things first in my life. I don't know how much time I have, so please, God, let me live in a way that pleases you so that I can complete well the purpose you have set for my life. Thank you for this day and that your mercies are new every morning. In Jesus' name, Amen.

40

WISDOM
IS BEING THERE

At the writing of this chapter, I have been sharing pearls of wisdom from Wyndham each week for a hundred weeks in various ways. I have been blessed with Wyndham's presence since his diagnosis of MSA. Each week is a blessing. Every day is a gift.

Over these past hundred weeks that I have been writing chapters for this book, God has been transforming my heart. The decline of Wyndham's health to the point he can do nothing for himself and my caring for him has transformed us both.

This week I've been reflecting on lessons learned as a caregiver. I was not looking to learn so many lessons, as neither of us willingly signed up for this class. From my early teen days as a candy striper (volunteer nurses' helper) at the hospital, I was confident that caregiving was not my thing. My very first assignment was to fill the patients' water pitchers with ice. Instead, I filled all their urinals. I had no idea until a man laughed and said to me, "This gives peeing on the rocks an entirely different meaning." I was so embarrassed.

Wisdom Is Being There

I don't like to lean into pain and suffering. I prefer to run the other way—but caregiving forces me to "be there." Really there. It's a constant reminder that Wyndham and I are temporarily here, though permanently homed with God. To live life in the fear of death is suffocating. I've felt that; however, the resurrection allows us to overcome this fear, though it's not easy. I'm not there yet but making good progress.

I would much rather fix Wyndham's suffering than enter it to stay. I can't cure, but I can certainly care. Through all the associated ups and downs, God has stayed with us. He has been present in our pain and participated in our joys. He hasn't left us alone and promises he never will. I am humbled that Jesus came here to lean into my pain and suffering in every way—to give me hope. To be with me. To hurt with me. To rejoice with me. To be present with me during my short time on this stage, as life truly is a mist. A good mist, however, full of inexpressible joys and unimaginable sorrows. Full of the warmth of love and the beauty of a creation that only God could imagine.

Wyndham, in such complete weakness, is still strong. Of course, he doesn't like being in his situation, but he graciously accepts it. He finds fullness in the presence of God and in the presence of those he dearly loves. This time has flushed out any pretense of identity. God's love and acceptance must always be enough. Suddenly, things I once felt important take an appropriate place. What we do is nothing compared to who we are—God's beloved. The important thing is to experience and to give that love.

As one who likes to stay busy, I can, at times, feel impatient with the slowness, repetitiveness, and tediousness of caregiving. Our home is our hospital, our restaurant, our theater, our vacation place, his church, my office, my schoolroom...but most importantly a place to give and receive love. It's a haven, yet I can at times feel guilty when I miss the freedom to be outside its borders.

In so many ways, this chapter of life is a gift. It seems strange to say this, as it's a gift I don't really want yet find precious—sort of sacred. Above all, I am learning the importance of just being by his side. I know how important my presence is to Wyndham because he can't do anything without me (or someone who is here caring for him). What a stark illustration this is to me of Jesus' words in John 15:5: "I am the vine; you are the branches. If you remain in me and I in you, you will bear much fruit; apart from me you can do nothing." I am completely helpless without the presence of Jesus in my life. Completely. But fortunately, I don't have to be apart from him.

God with us means everything. This is why Jesus is such an amazing gift to us. Emmanuel, God with us. This is the biggest lesson I am learning. Nothing is better than to be in his presence. It really is enough.

I have sweet memories of my mother (before she became deaf) singing in our home. One of her most oft-sung songs contained the words:

> Anywhere with Jesus, I can safely go,
> Anywhere he leads me in this world below.
> Anywhere without him, dearest joys would fade;
> Anywhere with Jesus, I am not afraid.
> Anywhere! anywhere! Fear I cannot know.
> Anywhere with Jesus I can safely go.

What a beautiful message that says Jesus is with us. His presence is everything. His presence is enough. Thank you, Jesus, for never leaving me alone.

Wisdom Is Being There

LORD, you alone are my portion and my cup;
> you make my lot secure.
The boundary lines have fallen for me in pleasant
> places;
> surely I have a delightful inheritance.
I will praise the LORD, who counsels me;
> even at night my heart instructs me.
I keep my eyes always on the LORD.
> With him at my right hand, I will not be shaken.
Therefore my heart is glad and my tongue rejoices;
> my body also will rest secure,
because you will not abandon me to the realm of
the dead,
> nor will you let your faithful one see decay.
You make known to me the path of life;
> *you will fill me with joy in your presence,*
> with eternal pleasures at your right hand. (Psalm
16:5–11, emphasis added)

Therefore go and make disciples of all nations, baptizing them in the name of the Father and of the Son and of the Holy Spirit, and teaching them to obey everything I have commanded you. And surely *I am with you always,* to the very end of the age." (Matthew 28:18–20, emphasis added)

FOR REFLECTION

What does it mean to you for God to be with you? How can you strengthen this relationship, so that you are more aware of him always? Consider praying through the Psalms, to better understand the meaning of his presence in your life and thoughts.

Father, my desire is to know and love you more deeply.

WEDNESDAYS WITH WYNDHAM

Please open wider the eyes of my heart so that I can see you more clearly and long, more than anything else, for your presence. Forgive me for my self-reliance and let me find joy in your presence. Thank you for being with me, as I live for you. In Jesus' name, Amen.

41

WISDOM TAKES RISKS

Years ago, Wyndham called from Bucharest saying he had met three abandoned siblings. They were alone, living in a shed with a dirt floor. He told me we needed to take them into our soon-to-open group home. For years we had worked toward the opening of this home in Romania, staffed by Christians. We would bring seventeen orphans, ages four to eight, from a state orphanage to live in the home. We knew we could not take more children than the ones that were already coming, and we knew that we could not take older children. There were just too many risks to an already risky undertaking.

So, when he called to tell me about these three children, ages ten to thirteen, I was not persuaded. I did not know how we could handle it, and besides, we didn't really know them. When he responded, "We need to do this; you are going to have to trust me on this one," I reluctantly agreed. After spending time with them, he saw through to their hearts and felt their needs. The oldest sibling had made sure they all took the very long route to school each day. Life in the shed where they lived abandoned was difficult, to say the least.

Wyndham convinced me that this was a risk we must take. So we did. They came to live in the home before the others came. Two girls and a boy. We celebrated Alex's

193

tenth birthday shortly after his arrival. He had never celebrated a birthday.

The day arrived when the seventeen kids were added to the home. The intensity of that first week is difficult to describe. I don't think I slept more than a few hours the whole week. On a level of difficulty between one and ten, it was near twenty. The oldest sibling from the shed was an outstanding "big sister" for all. All three of them were (are) wonderful. The oldest sibling, Ionela, was moved by the love she saw from the Christians. There were times when I saw her outside, off by herself reading the Bible. Over time, she fell in love with God. One of the great joys of my life was helping to baptize her in the home in Romania. After a couple of years, all three were adopted by good friends, the Rushtons, who gave them a wonderful home. Today, all three are married with children.

Ionela and her husband, Anthony, have four boys and both serve in the ministry in the Chicago area. She is truly an amazing woman. This past week we received a letter, which she graciously said I could share, so I will include excerpts:

> You have blessed my life. Thank you for saying "YES" to bringing my siblings and me to the group home. Because of your faith, sacrifice, love, and hard work my life has been changed for eternity. The group home is where I came to know God through the disciples and studying the Bible.

Wisdom Takes Risks

This past year I celebrated eighteen years as a disciple, more than half my life. That decision has changed everything. I got to marry a godly man who also had a dream to go into the full-time ministry, and together we have been serving in the ministry for ten years. We have been blessed with four amazing boys and we have the blessing to raise them to know and love God. My life and the blessings I enjoy every day are a result of your faith and sacrifice. Thank you for loving God first and letting him use you to change lives for eternity...

Wyndham, you are truly a man after God's own heart! Thank you for the incredible example of faith, courage, endurance, love, and sacrifice you have set for those around you and far away. As you have been suffering from your health you have become a stronger warrior. You both are warriors and your legacy is deep faith that has impacted many. I look forward to celebrating the reward of our faith with our God in our eternal home.

"I always thank my God as I remember you in my prayers." Philemon 1:4

I love you both very much, Ionela (Testa)

Okay, now my eyes are leaking. We never know what will happen when we listen to the Spirit's guidance and take a risk, even when that risk disturbs our plans. If we listen to all that could go wrong, we would never move forward. Wisdom takes risks.

I'm so glad Wyndham listened to the Spirit's guidance and took this risk. God certainly took a risk on me, and I am eternally grateful. He gave up everything in hopes that you and I would respond to his love. I want him to see my life and be happy that he took that risk.

> Out of that terrible travail of soul,
>> he'll see that it's worth it and be glad he did it.
> Through what he experienced, my righteous one,
>> my servant,
>> will make many "righteous ones,"
> as he himself carries the burden of their sins.
> (Isaiah 53:11 MSG)

FOR REFLECTION

Consider whether you are living your life for God in the comfort range. Jesus never lived his life "comfortably." What spiritual risk do you think God may be calling you to take? Pray to have the faith to take that risk.

Father, thank you that you took such a huge risk for me. You sent Jesus to die for me and gave me the freedom to choose my response. Help me to live by faith and not by sight. Show me the faith risks you desire me to take for you, Father, and help me to faithfully follow through.

42

WISDOM
LEARNS TO DANCE

Wyndham has many strengths. Dancing was never one of them. He just hears the beat of a different drummer. It's not that he didn't want to dance with the beat, he just didn't hear it. Our children have had fun in the past imitating his one and only dance move. It looked like the action movement that accompanies the children's song called "Roll the Gospel Chariot Along." The action consists of twirling one's hands around each other. Right there, that was Wyndham's dance move. (Oh, how I'd love to see that simple move now.)

So, it was particularly meaningful (and wise), when he agreed to take ballroom dance lessons with me for a couple of months preceding Sam and Leigh Ann's wedding fourteen years ago. I love to dance. When I hear music, I can't help myself. The rhythm makes me want to move. It makes me happy. It may not be pretty, but I do feel the beat of the

music and love to respond. For a few months, we, along with Sam and Leigh Ann, took ballroom dance lessons at an Arthur Murray studio that happened to be about a mile from our house. We all had fun, and since Wyndham can count quite well, we learned some basic 1,2,3,4 box steps. Sam and I, by contrast, had some "out of the box" steps at the wedding.

I recently passed by the now-closed studio and reminisced about that time and thought about dancing. I see a metaphor with dancing and a relationship with God. Too often, one's theology of Christianity means adherence to outward laws while under the observation of an "all-seeing eye" in the heavens. God is often wrongly perceived as uninvolved, too big to care, or too small to intervene. There could certainly be no "dancing" with such a God. Perhaps some think of Christianity as sitting in an audience watching God "perform," as the audience member can only watch in awe at the marvelous grace, majesty, and power of the dancer, not participate in the dance.

Too often, we view God as separated from us, the "audience," divided by the vast gulf of the orchestra pit. I picture my relationship with God as one in which Jesus crossed the gulf of the pit and—extending his hand to me, in the audience—carried me to the stage of life to dance

Wisdom Learns to Dance

with him. As I follow his lead, I begin to hear the music of God's orchestra and am better able to fall into step with his dance. I'm clumsy, so he starts me with the simple 1,2,3,4. I get tangled up in my own feet; however, I realize that when I trust him and let go of me, it's an exhilarating, scary, beautiful, unimaginable, thrilling, frightening, and oh-so-wonderful dance. He never lets me fall; I just have to hang on and follow his lead.

When the music portrays the sounds of tragedy, God lifts me; when the music elicits fear, God holds me; when I need to step out of my comfort zone, God twirls me; and when I can't hear the music, he guides me. For some reason, he wants to dance with me and invites me into partnership with him. He carried me over the pit that separated us, and as Zephaniah pens in 3:17:

> "The LORD your God is with you,
>   the Mighty Warrior who saves.
> He will take great delight in you;
>   in his love he will no longer rebuke you,
>   but will rejoice over you with singing."

I never want to be separated from him, because I'd fall into the pit, and on my own, I really can't dance. If I distance myself, I can't even hear his song. Oh, but this dance is not just for me. He is calling everyone to this dance, and it becomes more beautiful as it is synchronized, reflecting his grace and majesty. Everyone who joins has their own special dance moves to contribute. I want everyone I know to join in, so I invite as many as I can. I tell them to listen to his music (his words) and follow his lead in order to let him carry them across the pit to dance in step with his Spirit of grace and truth.

The beautiful truth is that God calls us into a relationship with him. I must be attentive, imitating his heart, vision, and purpose, to hear and follow him. God is not uninvolved with me or any of his creation; and in fact, his Spirit dwells in me. As Galatians 5:25 states, "Since we live by the Spirit, let us keep in step with the Spirit." Otherwise, we will "dance to the beat of a different drummer," with disastrous results. I long to listen to and obey the word of God, while understanding the freedom resulting in the dance God wants to dance with me. I remind myself that there is no fear in love (1 John 4:18) and that I can know and rely on the love God has for me (1 John 4:10). So I will keep on dancing, twirling, and holding on for dear life...all the way into heaven. Wisdom loves to dance.

Photo credit: lindacreates.com

FOR REFLECTION

Reflect on the Spirit of God in your life. How well do you keep in step with the Spirit? Have you accepted God's invitation to "dance" with you? What might this look like in your life today? Consider the scriptures above and pray that God will fill you with his Spirit in ever-increasing ways.

Father God, I thrill that you want to have a relationship with me. I am humbled and grateful. Help me to be more aware of your Spirit's promptings and help me to desire and strive to keep in step with your Spirit. Help me to grow in new ways today and every day as I strive to reflect you in ever-increasing measure. I long to feel the freedom of complete trust as you lead me in this dance. I love you and need you desperately. In Jesus' name, Amen.

43

WISDOM SITS

Is it possible to make a difference in someone's life just by sitting beside them? You may think, as you pull a chair beside someone, that you are just casually sitting by them, nothing more. "Just sitting" beside someone seemed insignificant to me for many years, but I have since learned its importance. This lesson concerning the importance of "just sitting" pierced my heart while in a stark and dingy hospital room in Romania during the late 1990s. The scene before me changed my worldview and gave me new, deepened convictions, compelling me to grow my heart. I was so struck that I captured the moment by photo (with an old-fashioned camera). I'll never forget this boy's dark hair and simple cap framing his sunken face. He was obviously

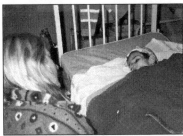

ill. I took this picture because I never wanted to forget him or the woman sitting beside him. My heart went out to this young boy, whose life would end before the day was over.

I wondered about the significance of the woman sitting beside him. I learned she was not related to the boy; she really didn't even know him. But in her travels she had seen children like him die alone, as orphans. She put her life in Ireland on hold and volunteered her time, simply by sitting alongside the sick children as they died. She believed that no one should have to die alone. My heart still swells with emotion as I write this memory.

In the Scriptures, we can read about Job's illness and suffering. Job's friends understood the importance of sitting beside their friend:

> When Job's three friends, Eliphaz the Temanite, Bildad the Shuhite and Zophar the Naamathite, heard about all the troubles that had come upon him, they set out from their homes and met together by agreement to go and sympathize with him and comfort him. When they saw him from a distance, they could hardly recognize him; they began to weep aloud, and they tore their robes and sprinkled dust on their heads. Then they sat on the ground with him for seven days and seven nights. No one said a word to him, because they saw how great his suffering was. (Job 2:11–13)

Job's friends acted fabulously—that is until they opened their mouths to explain all the reasons why Job was suffering. Then they became unhelpful and discouraging. They teach us valuable lessons. We must discern when it is best to talk and when it is more helpful to just sit and be with someone. Most of the time we don't know the reasons why someone is ill, except that we live in a temporary and fallen world. Let the one who is suffering give the cues as to what is most helpful and pray for discernment.

Wisdom comes when we take the time to listen in order to understand. When we do this, we will know better what to say and how to respond. Wyndham always excelled in

Wisdom Sits

this quality. When we practice this, we may even find ourselves, like the woman pictured, sitting with strangers. She saw a need, and out of the compassion in her heart, she responded.

I love to walk and talk with others. It is not as easy for me to sit and be silent; however, I have had to learn to do so through my current situation. Daily, when I transfer Wyndham to his hospital bed in our room for his late afternoon rest, I bring our big, black office chair into the room. From this chair, I feed him dinner when he awakes, and most every night from 9 PM until 1 AM, I can be found sitting in that chair beside his bed.  I am usually studying during this time while he watches something on television; thus, I am quiet except for inquiring about his needs. The important thing to him (and to me), is that I am sitting there beside him.

We are not alone. Not only does God sit with me (and Wyndham) as I sit beside the bed, but amazingly, I know that he has invited me to sit with him! This helps me to remember that these difficult times, for us all, are temporal. We have an amazing seat God has given us in the heavenly places. Yes, he has already given this to all who are Christians. This seat is not just reserved for life after death, but we can sit there now! From this seat, our perspective on caring, giving, and hope can be transformed to be like Christ's. May we all better comprehend the immeasurable and incomparable riches of his grace, expressed through Jesus' kindness to us.

WEDNESDAYS WITH WYNDHAM

But because of his great love for us, God, who is rich in mercy, made us alive with Christ even when we were dead in transgressions—it is by grace you have been saved. And God raised us up with Christ and seated us with him in the heavenly realms in Christ Jesus, in order that in the coming ages he might show the incomparable riches of his grace, expressed in his kindness to us in Christ Jesus. (Ephesians 2:4–7, emphasis added)

FOR REFLECTION

Consider times when God has sat with you. How does this make you feel? If you can't relate to God's sitting with you, reread and meditate on the above scripture, asking God to help you understand what it means to be seated with him in the heavenly realms. As you experience this security, think of ways you might pass this on to others as you sit with them.

Father, thank you for sitting beside me, even when I don't realize you are there. Help me to better grasp your presence and desire for relationship. Let me respond by holding nothing back from you, Father. You desire my all. You are my all. Help me, as a response to your unending love, to seek ways to give this love to others. Let me listen well. In Jesus' name, Amen.

44

WISDOM VALUES
THE DINNER TABLE

Amazing connections happen at the dinner table, but only if we actually sit and talk at the table. Has the "art of the dinner table" been lost? Do you value the dinner table? Wisdom values the dinner table. Or rather, what can happen around the table.

What happens at the dinner table? Unfortunately, the atmosphere can too often include technology, complaining, anger, and a downright mess. But dinner tables that are done right build family, connect with others, create precious memories, and prayerfully help the "diners" see God in action, resulting in a desire to grow in relationship with him.

Our family, for many decades, has taken a week in the summer for a family vacation. Since Wyndham can no longer travel, we have since enjoyed "staycations." It was fabulous, meaningful, and fun. We played, prayed, swam, did crazy Olympics, played tennis, played

cornhole, and gathered often around the dinner table. The crazy antics brought laughter and tears to Wyndham as he watched. This picture is from several years ago when he could still go outside.

Jesus was a firm believer in sharing meals. Matthew 11:19 tells us that Jesus came eating and drinking. He valued shared meals and realized the impact they have on all involved. He ate with sinners (Matthew 9:9–11) and invites us all to his feast (Matthew 22:4). He shared dinner with close friends (John 12:2), and in Luke 14 used the dinner table to teach valuable lessons.

Tonight, as our family of seventeen gathered around the dinner table, I asked the question, What happens at the dinner table? Here are some of their responses (from both kids and adults):

- We talk about the highs and lows of our days.
- We celebrate birthdays and victories or encourage someone who is discouraged.
- We laugh.
- We listen to each other and find out how everyone is doing.
- We encourage each other.
- We talk about our schedules.
- Sometimes we throw food (spoken for the 18-month-old).
- We have friends over to build relationships.
- We meet new people.
- We try new foods.
- We pray.

Wyndham has always valued and protected our dinner table. Over the years we have built family around the dinner

Wisdom Values the Dinner Table

table. We've explored emotions. Laughed. Cried. Shared fears. Shared victories. Shared defeats. Truthfully, every mealtime wasn't like this. Sometimes they were hurried, sometimes someone was moody or distracted—but the sum of the times around the table added up to the love, warmth, and family-feel that linger with us.

Our dinner table has also seated many a neighbor or acquaintance, who often shared that they had never before been invited to dinner with a neighbor. Many Bible studies began at the dinner table, resulting in changed lives.

Wanderers from the faith (mainly because of Wyndham's persistent desire to see hearts restored to God) have felt loved, welcomed, and safe around the dinner table. I can think of numerous men and women who were helped back to God because of Wyndham's commitment to using Monday evenings to have dinner with some who had wandered from their faith.

Something happens around the table as we connect with one other. The senses of taste, sound, smell, and sight somehow morph together to imprint on our hearts, leaving us with a feeling of love and belonging—family. Jesus knew this and realized that sharing meals together would reveal hearts, melt hearts, and capture memories. He shared many such meals with his closest friends as well as with strangers and sinners. These meals helped them never forget his love and call to follow him. We still remember him  together through communion, which by definition is not

WEDNESDAYS WITH WYNDHAM

an individual or solo activity.

Wisdom knows that the dinner table is powerful. It doesn't have to be pretty to "do its thing." But it must be filled with love.

May we all create such dinner tables as we follow Jesus' example.

FOR REFLECTION

Reflect on a time you have spent with someone around a loving dinner table. How did it make you feel? How might you more consistently offer hospitality, bringing others around your dinner table?

Loving God, thank you that you have made a place for me at your table. Help me have the vision and faith to create a loving dinner table for others, no matter what I have experienced in the past. Help me to both learn and to give in order that I might practice hospitality in a way that reflects your love and kindness, and help me to follow through on my desire to do so. In Jesus' name, Amen.

45

WISDOM BUILDS FAMILY

It's one thing to love the special people in your life. It's another to help those you love to love each other; yet this is what building family means. Jesus' great desire, expressed in John 17, is that his family would love each other. Family, based on and flowing from God's love and unity, can show God's love to the world.

"My prayer is not for them alone. I pray also for those who will believe in me through their message, that all of them may be one, Father, just as you are in me and I am in you. May they also be in us so that the world may believe that you have sent me. I have given them the glory that you gave me, that they may be one as we are one—I in them and you in me—so that they may be brought to complete unity. Then the world will know that you sent me and have loved them even as you have loved me." (John 17:20–23)

Jesus expressed a similar thought earlier in John 13:34–35.

"A new command I give you: Love one another. As I have loved you, so you must love one another. By this everyone will know that you are my disciples, if you love one another."

Wyndham had great determination and ability to build family—both in our immediate family as well as with work colleagues, friends, small groups, and churches. This did not happen by accident. It was nurtured, purposely. He was convinced that joy multiplied when those we love, love each other. That's how unity is built.

Our family loves spending time together. I mean, we really love it. We are best friends with each other, including in-laws. The cousins (our grandkids) are best friends. Beyond the family, I am also grateful for our friendships and the partnerships we share communally.

So how does building family happen? Do loving relationships happen because certain individuals are exceptionally compatible? Does it happen randomly or accidentally? I don't think so. As I think through qualities and characteristics that have helped to build family, several values important to Wyndham also stand out to me, which include:

- *Making special times to be together* – Whether it was the two of us, the immediate family, a work staff, or some other group, Wyndham set (and kept) times to be together—and asked for others to set apart time as well. For the family growing up, these times included the daily dinner table, weekly family devotionals, and yearly vacations—getting away together. For others, it was various kinds of gatherings. Those times together built lasting memories.
- *Building memories* – Having fun together, laughing together, sharing in each other's special events, reminiscing, and crying together

Wisdom Builds Family

are all part of building family. We deliberately pulled each other into these times. (No one left behind.) I'm so grateful for the memories and the pictures (and for those who remembered to take pictures). Memories live on. Even though Wyndham can no longer "do" much, he can remember, pray, laugh, and cry with the others in his life.

- *Expressing love and affection* – Affection is not my first love language; mine is all about acts of service. However, affection is one of Wyndham's love languages, and I have learned from him how affection helps people feel loved. Wyndham is a great giver of hugs and taught our kids to be affectionate; thus, whenever anyone comes or goes—beginning with the youngest grandkids—hugs are given and received. Affection makes a difference; there is even data describing the way affection improves our quality of life. We also celebrate every birthday by sharing something we love about the birthday person. Though we grow older, this practice never gets old.

- *A shared purpose and love for our heavenly Father* – Through praying together as a group, serving the poor together, sharing our faith together (and at times borrowing each other's faith) we build family, physically and spiritually.

- *Expressing and resolving qualms and hurts* – Every family will have misunderstandings, hurts, and "bumps" (which is a kind word for fights). No family or group is without sin or "stupidity." Wyndham never lets hurts or qualms go unresolved. Grace and forgiveness are crucial for building any family. Whenever someone felt something, Wyndham would dig until they could express what they felt inside. With practice, this grew easier and became customary for them.

Wisdom helps those we love to love each other. May we be wise as we lovingly interact in order to build family in our homes, churches, and even our workplaces.

To offer a deeper look into building family, the following chapters are written by family members. Most of them were written several years ago. As we are growing older, unfortunately, Wyndham's disease is progressing. Through it all, we are a family that loves each other. I now invite you into our home in order to share more of what family means to us and ways Wyndham's wisdom affected our entire family.

Wisdom Builds Family

FOR REFLECTION

What qualities make you feel "at home" with someone? In which of the keys to building family mentioned above will you choose to make progress?

Abba, thank you that you took human form in Jesus to show me what it means to love. Help me to be so close to you that I can, by your Spirit, help others to love each other. Help me to love as Jesus loved so that I can grow in building my physical family and my spiritual family. Thank you that no matter what kind of family I experienced, you love me perfectly and allow me to love others as you have loved me. I need your love and power to grow. I thank you for making me part of your family. In Jesus' name, Amen.

46

WISDOM WEARS
A BLUE ROBE

by Sam Shaw

If you were to walk into the Shaw house at 6:30 AM on a weekday in the year 2000 you would undoubtedly encounter the following: 1) two slightly toasted chocolate Pop-Tarts, 2) a sleeping seventeen-year-old on the living room floor holding his untied shoelaces, and 3) my dad in a blue robe reading the Bible on the living room couch.

I'm not a robe guy, but my dad is. Every morning during my high school years he customarily wore a blue one with his initials embroidered on the section covering his left chest. Although I cringed imagining him wearing it in public, that robe holds significant meaning to me.

Apparently, God is also a blue-robe fan. He commanded Aaron to wear a blue robe while serving as high priest in the Jewish tabernacle in Exodus 39. Needless to say, wearing the blue robe involves weighty spiritual obligations and accountability. As his son, I have a uniquely close-up view of how my dad manages his "blue-robe" responsibilities as a spiritual leader.

My dad and I frequently have deep conversations now that our relationship involves less football throwing and golf club swinging. During one recent conversation, he

Wisdom Wears a Blue Robe

commented that highly talented people often have fatal flaws and that both success and failure will expose these flaws if a person lacks integrity. If you're reading this book, there's no need to sell you on my dad's exceptional spiritual leadership abilities. I've closely witnessed his highest highs and lowest lows as a spiritual leader. My conclusion: I have not known nor will I ever know a man of greater integrity. He's perfectly suited for the blue robe.

For me, the image of my dad reading the Bible in his blue robe embodies why I hold him in higher regard than any other human. First and foremost, it validates his exceptionally authentic faith. He teaches, preaches, and encourages people to devote themselves to God and others above self, and his morning routine during those years tangibly represented how he privately practiced what he publicly preached. It's uncommon to see someone clearly proclaim biblical truth without compromise, and even more scarce to see someone live it out. I took my dad's exceptional integrity for granted early in life. Our world is inherently skeptical of authority figures, understandably so considering how often they abuse power, act out of self-interest, seem apathetic, or are simply incompetent to handle their responsibilities. Because of my dad's example, I have an abnormally positive outlook on authority and leadership. He has made it easy for me to recognize how great it is to be under God's authority.

Second, the blue robe inspired my personal faith. My dad's consistent morning time reading the Bible, often with brief interruptions so he could share something he was learning with me, drove me to seek an individual connection with his God. My dad never wanted me to be just like him; he wanted me to experience, as he had, a real, true, and fulfilling relationship with our Creator. It struck me how tangible an invisible God was to him, and that the Bible actually directed the way he lived his life; so much so that I felt an urge, not an obligation, to explore it for myself.

Finally, the blue robe represents his approachability. I find it hard to believe when people say my dad intimidates them. Trust me, the corny robe/bed head combination does not create a threatening vibe. He commands much respect, but I never felt afraid of my dad. Long before he donned the robe of my high school years, his selfless pursuit of my friendship, willingness to share his weaknesses, and gentle instruction removed all fear from our relationship. 1 John 4:18 says, "There is no fear in love. But perfect love drives out fear." I can talk to my dad about anything and feel safe, yet he'll never hold back the truth, even if it's hard to handle. I've only observed Jesus have this skill in greater measure than my dad, no one else.

James 1:2–4 says it's pure joy to face many trials because they test our faith and produce perseverance, which makes us mature and complete. My dad's current physical condition is a trial of the highest order, one that he faces with unimaginable joy and grace as he reaches heights of

Wisdom Wears a Blue Robe

maturity few could imagine, let alone attain. Quite fitting, if you ask me, for a man who wears a blue robe.

FOR REFLECTION

What does it mean to you to possess integrity? How would those closest to you describe your integrity? Consider a way you can grow to gain deeper integrity.

Father, you are worthy of all respect. You are the definition of integrity, keeping your promises to a thousand generations. Forgive me when I fail you, and help me be a person of integrity. May my thoughts, meditation, and actions be pleasing to you from the inside out. Show me the areas of duplicity in my heart and help me to live fully devoted to you. Help me to guard my heart above all else, knowing all issues of my life spring from my heart. In Jesus' name, Amen.

47

WISDOM ENCOURAGES

by Leigh Ann Shaw

> Your love has given me great joy and encouragement, because you, brother, have refreshed the hearts of the Lord's people. (Philemon 1:7)

I have the privilege of carrying the same last name as Wyndham, as I married into the Shaw family. Not only am I beyond blessed to have Sam as my husband, but I also have the most amazing in-laws who love me and have taught me so much.

It is difficult to share just one thing I have learned from Wyndham because I could share many. He is a man of great strength and dignity, yet he is humble and meek. He is a man of deep conviction and has a wealth of knowledge, yet he is eager to learn from others.

Wyndham is in a stage of life where he could be focused on himself and his own needs, yet he looks for ways to encourage others. As his daughter-in-law, I am very fortunate to receive an abundance of encouragement from Wyndham.

Wisdom Encourages

I remember one day when I was in the throes of motherhood with a five-year-old, a three-year-old, and a newborn. I was feeling particularly overwhelmed by a lack of sleep and the many tasks at hand. Satan was throwing his flaming arrows at me. Thoughts like "You're an incompetent mom," "You lack value," and "You are not good enough" were swarming through my head that day. As I was departing from a family party, I hugged Wyndham to tell him goodbye. He held me a little tighter and a little bit longer and said, "I love you. You're a great mom and I'm grateful for the wife you are to my son."

My eyes filled up with tears as I walked away (and as they are right now). He spoke words of encouragement that touched my soul. Wyndham's words remind me of a scripture in Hebrews 3:13: "But encourage one another daily, as long as it is called 'Today,' so that none of you may be hardened by sin's deceitfulness."

While I strive every day to remember God's love for me and to get my security and confidence from him, Satan is a strong enemy and his flaming arrows of lies come to attack every day. It is refreshing to have someone help deflect those arrows. Wyndham does this for me and for many others. I want to imitate his example and encourage others daily as he does.

FOR REFLECTION

Determine to notice people and listen to them as you go through your day today. Everyone experiences challenges and difficulties. Commit to intentionally speak encouragement to someone today.

Father, you are the God of encouragement as you speak through creation, through your word, through your

WEDNESDAYS WITH WYNDHAM

Holy Spirit, and through your people. Use me as an instrument of encouragement. Help me notice and listen well so that I might show love and compassion to someone today. In Jesus' name, Amen.

48

WISDOM IMPARTS
CONFIDENCE FROM GOD

by Kristen Shaw Gonet

Several years ago my husband and I and our two children left Massachusetts where I lived five minutes away from my parents and moved to an affluent town in central Connecticut. It's the kind of town in which, though I'm thirty-six years old, I can still find myself trying to keep up with the "popular crowd." I have watched the pressure my children face to compete to be in the highest reading group in their class, and their struggle when they are not the best on their team at a sport or not wearing the right clothes. It is overwhelming to try to keep up appearances in my community, but I can even feel that same pressure sometimes as a Christian. Am I serving enough? Giving enough? Have I done all my Christian duties? Being a wife, mom, Christian, and friend can sometimes feel like a never-ending checklist.

While I was growing up, I noticed that my dad never let life become a list of duties. His Christianity was

never a checklist; it was and still is his identity. Although I wanted badly just to fit in with the rest of the crowd when I was in high school, he constantly reminded me by the way he lived his life that the only ones with whom I needed to fit in were my parents and God. My dad's example was so powerful that I never actually had to wrestle with this worldly desire. He made sure I knew I fit perfectly next to him. When I was next to him, I was never afraid. He was a protector. Next to him, I didn't have to look a certain way because I never doubted that to him, I was beautiful. To him, I was strong, funny, a fighter, and smart. Now that I'm raising my own daughter, I understand in a way I never could before what a profound gift he gave me.

He has a sixth sense as a dad. He always knew (and still knows) whenever my sister and I caught a case of "daddy-itis." He could sense we were "off" and that we needed time with him. For the two of us, that usually meant a trip to Dunkin' Donuts followed by a long, often tear-filled conversation in the driveway talking about everything we were feeling at the time. He would listen to me talk about my current unrequited crush. He would then express to me his own disappointments. He never settled for an "I'm fine" response from me when he would ask me how I was doing. He would ask more questions or just sit and wait while we drank our hot chocolate until I was ready to talk. He would let me go on for hours about the trials of being a girl in middle school with bad acne. Nothing was off-limits, and I was never too embarrassed to tell him all the details. It may have been the six sisters he grew up with that gave him such a sensitive heart, but he somehow found a way to relate to me. I always felt listened to and understood. He would ultimately bring all of our con-

Wisdom Imparts Confidence from God

versalions back to Jesus and the Bible. He made Jesus and the Bible so real in those moments. I still cling to those talks.

In the busyness of life, I can often want to settle for the "I'm fine" responses from my kids or from my neighbors, but I think I inherited my dad's emotional intelligence and I can't help but dig deeper. I want to give my kids what my dad gave me. My daughter and I recently read Psalm 139 together. I want her to have the same confidence in who she is that my dad gave me, and I want her to know the true source from which it came. I watched her eyes fill with confidence as she thought about the fact that God made her just as he wanted! When I look at those around me I want to see beyond the "I'm all set" exterior and remember that people just need to be asked the right questions, or that sometimes they just need someone to sit and drink hot chocolate with them.

This world is full of broken people who need Jesus and the Bible to be made real in their lives. Dad is my hero and most trusted adviser. Although his voice is softer and he has less strength than he used to, his words remain just as loud in my heart, and his strength is just as profound as it was in his health.

For Reflection

Consider whether you are willing to go deep with your own emotions or with those of others. Do you settle for

WEDNESDAYS WITH WYNDHAM

saying "I'm fine" when you really aren't? Do you take time to draw others out? Reflect on ways to become more vulnerable both in your words and in compassionate listening with others.

Father, thank you that you considered me in my mother's womb and made me who I am. Help me to gain my true value from you and thus be willing to share the deepest parts of my soul with you and with others. Help me to care enough to notice others' pain and hurts and to offer them your love, which is always enough. Thank you for being my perfect Father. Amen.

49

WISDOM IMPARTS VALUES

by Justin Gonet

A month or so ago, my family and I stayed at the Shaw house for a weekend, as we often do these days. That Saturday night Wyndham wanted to teach my son, Micah, an impromptu lesson about fishing—to impart the tenets of the sport that's been a big part of his life from an early age.

The scene that ensued was mildly heart-wrenching—my father-in-law there in his wheelchair in the living room, his grandson on a child-sized yellow folding chair in front of him with his yellow note pad in hand, taking in every word and jotting down the key points. While my wife fought back tears, I gathered that there was an intense expression of love transpiring between master and pupil.

Wyndham is passionate about fishing. If you could watch him in action on a boat with a rod and reel in his hands, you would soon realize his love of the sport goes far beyond a hobby. His drawn-out fishing trips with his friends and family are a thing of legend.

What is amazing about Wyndham is that as he loved fishing so much and similarly loved people, he couldn't help but want others to participate with him. He found so much joy in fishing that he didn't really care what you thought of it, he just wanted you to experience it too! Fishing brought a sense of peace and freedom that drove him—in the midst of the waves and the shouting of orders at lesser mates. I've never seen such a thing before, nor have I ever been able to achieve it personally. I believe he understood there was a deeper, intrinsic value in fishing than just the sport itself. It brought a comradery. It seemed the longer and more arduous the trip, the deeper the bonds that eventually developed.

But as I watched my son in the midst of this lesson, I sensed there was something else going on. Wyndham was now trying to pass on to my son what he believed was of utmost importance. There was something about this sport he has enjoyed for so many years that he felt he had to pass on to Micah, even after his own ability to participate has left him.

Wyndham loves to pass things on. Recently, we acquired two fishing poles from his vast collection for Micah's further benefit. A few years ago Wyndham bought a chainsaw and became a bit of a traveling woodcutter-for-hire in order to boost his firewood stock. This past Christmas I received a new chainsaw as a gift from him, and an unwritten invitation to pick up where he had left off. Eight years ago, when his own dog, Jordan, was growing "long in the tooth," he brought golden retriever puppies home from Colorado for my family and Sam's family so we could train them in Jordan's shadow.

Having lived with my wife for over ten years now, I'm beginning to realize the breadth of Wyndham's ability to impart all that he is. He is a peerless dad to his kids. My

Wisdom Imparts Values

wife's ferocious loyalty to him is a testament to this. Much of how we love and discipline our children is based on the example that was set by him, long before I ever met him.

There is one thing Wyndham is even more passionate about delivering to others than fishing or family, and that is the gospel. In 1 Corinthians 15:3–4 the Bible says, "For what I received I passed on to you as of first importance: that Christ died for our sins according to the Scriptures, that he was buried, that he was raised on the third day according to the Scriptures..."

For over forty years, he has sought to embody the simple facts that Paul spells out in this scripture. The gospel is hard to believe; to live by it is an even more difficult calling. It is not a popular opinion; it is a narrow road. Wyndham's life's work has been to pass the gospel on to others. But beyond that, he's helped me understand that the gospel is so powerful it must pervade every aspect of our lives once we receive it. It is not only the path of our salvation, but it becomes our code of conduct until that salvation is realized in the end. It is our source of faith but also our ability to forgive; it is our hope in the life to come, but it defines the way we treat others now. The gospel is of first importance in every way.

For all of the great spiritual victories that my father-in-law has accomplished in his life, some of his most powerful stuff has been transferred in just the last few years, while in his weakest physical condition. I see the gospel being lived out in the most real way through the joy he still has, though he's been stripped of his ability to perform the most basic physical tasks—much less fishing and hunting.

I now understand that those things pale in comparison to the hope he has because of the gospel. I have seen no more powerful an example of the reality of the gospel truths than the way Wyndham has endured the pain and loss his disease has brought him.

As I listened to him wrap up his instruction on fishing, I was struck by the fact that even in the act of imparting his tidbits of wisdom, he had conveyed the most profound lesson about the gospel to my son.

For Reflection

What legacy do you want to leave to your family, friends, and colleagues? Consider what legacy your lifestyle and words currently impart. How might you more intentionally impart the wisdom of God to others?

Father, thank you for imparting yourself to me through Jesus and your Spirit. As I drink in your love, joy, peace, and all the fruits of your Spirit, help me to pass these on to others. Help me to be devoted to doing your will, so that I might impart the values that are most important to all around me. In Jesus' name, Amen.

50

WISDOM
MAKES GOD OUR STRENGTH

by Melissa Shaw Miller

I have to confess that as a little girl I often pretended to be asleep so that my dad would carry me in from the car or from the couch and put me to bed. Burying my head into his chest with my arms around his neck and my legs as limp as a rag doll's, I remember breathing in the gentle spice of his Brut aftershave, which will to me always be the fragrance of strong, safe, Dad—and of home. I have never felt a safer place in my life than being carried in the strength of my dad's arms.

Just the other day my eight-year-old daughter was rummaging through my husband's dresser to find just the right T-shirt of his to wear to bed. I smiled and savored the moment as I recounted how many times I wanted nothing else to wear to bed but my dad's T-shirts, because they were his and because being in bed clothed in something that was "him" made me sleep sweetly and securely.

From the earliest moments of being a little girl carried in from the car, to being lifted on his shoulders as a schoolgirl so that I could see over the crowds at a parade, to my teenage years with frizzy hair, braces, acne, and lonely times when his shoulder bore my tears, to the embraces before he dropped me off at college, to him walking me down the aisle on his arm and later dancing with me to "Butterfly Kisses," to him holding my own baby for the first time in his arms, he has constantly carried me through life.

By myself, I am naturally a guilty person who loves to think of ways I should've been or what I could've said, or what I would've done and how I'll never measure up to what I think is the mark of "rightness." I can be fearful and anxious, compare myself to others, and find the ways something can't be done. But from my first remembrances, I've had a real-life "championer" of me as he would tell me how it could be done, and how I am enough, valued, and worth it. This has clothed me in confidence and created the safest place. It has allowed me to let go and be carried by a far greater strength than my own.

My dad, almost every time he sees me, tells me how proud he is of me and expresses the good he sees in me, how valuable I am to him, and that he loves me. There have been so many moments when life has felt unfair, when people have left, when I have had no idea what I felt, when friends have moved, or it's been just plain hard to see the truth and I feel sad. My dad has the most uncanny way of drawing out my heart, listening intently as if I am the only human on the planet, empathizing in the most profound way, and hugging so it melts me, yet also gently carrying me back to what is right and good.

Life rarely happens as we plan it, and there are many things that can cause me to trip, stumble, and fall. Whether it was a scraped knee, a more impressive bike accident, or

Wisdom Makes God Our Strength

broken bones, the memories I have of my dad carrying me through my tears are far greater than the pain.

It's the yellow sticky notes of encouragement he stuck to the coffee pot in the early hours of the morning, written to give me the strength to keep walking with God, that I remember far more than the temporary high school crisis I was facing. It's the voice on the other end of the line telling me that it would be okay that stayed with me a hundred times more than whatever difficult problem distressed me.

What amazes me most about him is that through the most difficult challenges of his most cruel disease, he continues to carry me. I think one of the most impressive pieces of wisdom I have gained from this amazing man, who I get to call my dad, is his strength to let me go, and let God be who ultimately carries me and us.

He would give me every one of his T-shirts in a heartbeat, but what he most cares about and through tears has implored, is that he in no way wants the security that he provides to overshadow the ultimate rock, refuge and "carrier" that God is for me—or for me to forget that ultimately God is who will carry us home.

I have always felt the luckiest and most blessed that I get to be his daughter. He is immensely humble, inexpressibly kind and gentle, selfless beyond measure, mightily wise, and the strongest man that I know. I am very grateful for his T-shirts and I will cherish the days of wrapping my arms around his neck as hard as I could squeeze, but the wisdom he has imprinted on my heart (and the hearts of my children) to make God my refuge is eternally more profound.

> I love you, O LORD, my strength.

> The LORD is my rock, my fortress and my deliverer;
>   my God is my rock, in whom I take refuge,
>   my shield and the horn of my salvation, my
>   stronghold. (Psalm 18:1–2)

FOR REFLECTION

Consider times and ways that God has been your rock, your strength, and your deliverer. Thank him for those times and ways, and commit the above verse to memory.

> *Father, you alone are trustworthy and faithful. You are always good and have a perfect, eternal plan for my life. Help me to trust your plan, knowing that no one and nothing else is worthy or able to be my rock, strength, fortress, deliverer, and refuge. There is salvation in no one else. Let me hold fast to your presence and your word. Thank you for being my solid rock. I need you desperately and thank you for your unfailing love. Amen.*

51

WISDOM
FINDS SPIRITUAL HEROES

by Kevin Miller

Several months ago I was on the phone helping a friend and fellow disciple with his marriage—communication, emotional intelligence, patience—this kind of stuff. This brother and I had known each other in the faith for over two decades, and after helping him I felt satisfied that I had done a good job in the conversation. The feeling of self-satisfaction was short-lived though, as my friend commented, "Boy, I sure am glad you married into Wyndham's family; otherwise you would never know how to help with this kind of stuff!" I smiled on the other end of the line, humbly knowing that this was most certainly true.

And this is true of many areas of my life. The challenge of writing one chapter on the wisdom that Wyndham has passed on to me is that he has passed on so much. Is there an area of my life that he hasn't touched? I couldn't tell if there is one.

I met Wyndham in Paris. I was twenty-two years old and had just finished taking his daughter out on our first date. I think I was petrified to speak to him, as any young dreamer would be in front of a hero whom they'd heard so much about. Two years later, his daughter, Melissa, and I would marry. Since then, two decades of life have flown by.

Over the course of that time babies came, more in-laws, more babies, spiritual victories, church crises, family vacations, buying homes, selling homes, successes, failures, and lots of life. Through it all, Wyndham has gone from the intimidating hero of a young man to a mentor, trusted adviser, father figure, coworker, partner, friend, and ultimately the best of friends.

Throughout the last decade there has been very little we did not talk about—family, personal challenges, parenting, marriage, the Kingdom, Jesus, and church-building from every angle. I cherish it all. Who am I that I have gotten to sit at the feet, or in the fishing boat, of this man? (Although in the boat there is surprisingly less conversation that you might think; fishing with Wyndham was more intense than you might expect fishing could be.)

If forced to narrow down one piece of wisdom from my time with Wyndham I would share that this world needs spiritual heroes. If you were to ask my son for Wyndham's favorite scripture he would tell you:

> The goal of this command is love, which comes from a pure heart, a good conscience and a sincere faith. (1 Timothy 1:5)

A spiritual hero is a man who takes care of these three areas of his inner life. He protects his heart, maintains a biblically led conscience, and is authentic as he does it.

Wisdom Finds Spiritual Heroes

Over the course of Wyndham's life, he has modeled this and has encouraged me to do the same. This is the kind of man the world needs, and it's the kind of man he has been for over four decades.

Wyndham was a young evangelist in the 1970s. He was the first campus minister sent from the Crossroads campus ministry to see God bring over a hundred baptisms in one year on one campus. From the day that I met him, he has been a radical man filled with radical convictions.

Wyndham is also an elder extraordinaire. His deep impact in this area is felt worldwide. I have long observed that when people are hurting, when their marriage is in trouble, when they can't figure out their kids, Wyndham is on the short, shortlist of men that people call. And he helped to establish elderships filled with these kinds of men, literally all over the world.

It is in this blend of radical man and understanding shepherd that I have found Wyndham's wisdom. He has sought to imitate Jesus' grace and truth.

> We have seen his glory, the glory of the one and only Son, who came from the Father, full of grace and truth. (John 1:14b)

As I get older, I feel increasingly challenged by the fact that Jesus was the perfect balance of God's glory, full of both grace and truth. Many of us naturally gravitate toward one aspect of Jesus' character. Perhaps we are a naturally compassionate person, or maybe we are someone who embodies the revolutionary side of Jesus' personality—turning tables and confronting sin. Jesus was full of both grace and truth, two characteristics that seem diametrically opposed to one another. But in Jesus, they both took root equally well.

Unhealthy extremes exist in all corners, in the world and in the church. The amazing thing about Jesus was that he was the perfect blend of so many qualities you might think could not exist in the same man. He was filled with zeal, but also touched the leper. He drove the buyers and sellers out of the temple taking a whip to their animals but also wept over Jerusalem.

Wyndham comes closer to the Jesus blend than anyone else I've met. He believes in risk-taking, Kingdom-seeking examples of faith—and that churches need to be raising young people up, sending them out, and giving them responsibilities. But he also believes that we must be wise and compassionate, considering others' needs and being led by the humility of older men. He believes in strong and authoritative leadership, but also in consensus leadership and listening to the words, needs, and feelings of people. He believes in strong leaders but also in deep relationships.

It has always struck me how easy it is for big personalities with big gifts to do what they do and to shut out voices different from theirs. That's not what I've learned from Wyndham's wisdom. His deep love for Jesus and for the word of God have led him to strive to build a life and a church that glorifies, obeys, and follows God in all the areas God commands, not just the ones that are easy for him. Because of this, he is a unifier. He has been a leading voice in his generation during his sojourn here on earth. I strive to imitate these qualities of Jesus I see shining through his life as he serves as my spiritual hero.

Wisdom Finds Spiritual Heroes

FOR REFLECTION

How much care do you give your inner life as you strive for a pure heart, clear conscience, and sincere faith? Soul care takes time alone with God, learning from him, listening to his Spirit, and seeking his presence. There are no shortcuts. Evaluate the priority you give to your inner life with God and ways you will determine to strengthen it.

Father, I know there is nothing I can do outwardly that matters if my heart is not fully yours. Help me to guard my heart with all diligence, knowing everything else stems from this. I pray that my conscience will always be clear, with no secret sin. Create in me a pure heart, God, that I might serve you wholeheartedly for your sake, without selfish intent. I pray that my life will be authentic, open, and vulnerable as I follow you individually and in community. I need you every hour, Father. Thank you for Jesus, showing me a life of true integrity. I long to be more and more like him. In his name, Amen.

52

WISDOM TRUSTS

Our youngest son, Jacob, now thirty-three, grew up in a Romanian orphanage until he became part of our family at age twelve. He helped with Wyndham's caregiving, using his incredible physical strength to completely lift Wyndham once he could no longer move his body. When I wrote this, Wyndham could still help with transfers and we all learned great lessons on trust, something Jacob had never known as a child. Below is a short, poignant conversation between them when Wyndham could still talk and help in the transfers.

Jacob: You know Dad, I could lift you much easier if you would let go of the bar.

Wyndham: Sorry, I keep forgetting to let go.

Jacob: Dad, you can let go. I will never, ever drop you.

They laugh. I turn my head to hide the mist forming in my eyes.

"I will never, ever drop you." A tender moment. A big lesson. A profound expression of love and trust.

It takes trust, a whole lot of it, to let go of control—in transfers, and in life. The transferee (Wyndham) has absolutely no control over these moves and is at the mercy of those transferring him.

Wisdom Trusts

The three of us—Wyndham, Jacob, and I—meet for "transfer tasks" several times a day. We work together any time Wyndham must get from his bed or chair to anywhere else. Wyndham assists as much as he can, pulling himself forward to be lifted while holding on to a grab bar. Jacob can lift him completely but finds it quite difficult if Wyndham forgets to let go of the grab bar.

Such is life—and trust in God. Life these days hasn't gone as planned or hoped. Trust takes on new meanings—believing God loves us when our prayers are not answered in the ways we hope. Learning to trust through adversity stretches our faith and deepens our hope. The Scriptures express this well:

> Not only so, but we also glory in our sufferings, because we know that suffering produces perseverance; perseverance, character; and character, hope. And hope does not put us to shame, because God's love has been poured out into our hearts through the Holy Spirit, who has been given to us.
>   You see, at just the right time, when we were still powerless, Christ... (Romans 5:3–6)

I hold on to this scripture. Hope will never disappoint us. Because God has poured out his love.

And...when we are powerless...Christ!

When we realize we are powerless, God takes over as if saying, "Son, daughter...I will never, ever drop you."

> For I am the LORD your God,
>   who takes hold of your right hand
> and says to you, Do not fear;
>   I will help you. (Isaiah 41:13)

I watch with deep respect as I see Wyndham's wisdom in his decision to trust...and let go. He has had to let go of all that was normal and daily for him. In all of this, his trust grows. His trust inspires my trust.

When life doesn't go as planned, and difficulties happen—will you let go of the bar?

When life is going well—will you let go of the bar?

Our grasp for control makes it difficult for God to carry us. He won't force us. We have to let go. Often this is a struggle, as we learn from the psalms:

> How long must I wrestle with my thoughts
>   and day after day have sorrow in my heart?
> How long will my enemy triumph over me?
>
>   Look on me and answer, LORD my God.
> Give light to my eyes, or I will sleep in death,
> and my enemy will say, "I have overcome him,"
>   and my foes will rejoice when I fall.
>
> But I trust in your unfailing love;
>   my heart rejoices in your salvation.
> I will sing the LORD's praise,
>   for he has been good to me.
> (Psalm 13:2–6, emphasis added)

When we were powerless...Christ.

God is big enough, strong enough, and loving enough to hold us, no matter what.

He tells us, "I will never, ever drop you."

Wisdom trusts.

Wisdom Trusts

FOR REFLECTION

In what area(s) in your life do you find it hardest to trust God? What does it look like in your life when you try to take control? What do you think trusting God would look like in your life? What would be different?

Father, I know in my mind you are big enough, loving enough, and strong enough to completely carry my burdens, all of them. I believe, Lord; help my unbelief. Help me to trust you with everything in my life, letting go of anxious thoughts concerning things I cannot control. Help me every day to trust you from the depths of my heart, understanding more and more your love for me. Thank you that you, alone, are trustworthy and will never let me go. Help me to never let go of you, Father. In Jesus' name, Amen.

53

WISDOM
Passes the Torch

...things we have heard and known,
 things our ancestors have told us.
We will not hide them from their descendants;
 we will tell the next generation
the praiseworthy deeds of the Lord,
 his power, and the wonders he has done.
(Psalm 78:3–4)

Our grandchildren, now ages three to seventeen, were indescribable sources of joy for Wyndham. I believe part of the reason he lived as long as he did was his desire to see them grow up. His greatest sadness came knowing he would not be able to watch them grew older (at least from the perspective he knew on earth). When first gathering chapters for this book several years ago, the four oldest grandchildren were quick to write chapters. The following paragraphs are excerpts from their contributions.

Wisdom Passes the Torch

My grandfather blows me away with his faith. The way he handles the health challenges he goes through, the way he teaches people, the way he loves people...and I could go on. Several years ago, while on vacation with him and my family, I had the opportunity to sit down and talk with him for a while, listening to his life story and hearing pieces of his wisdom. I had prepared a list of questions for him. He talked to me about the way he stays hopeful and rooted in Jesus as his foundation—no one else. He keeps his eyes on eternal life, not this earthly life...although he's had it to the full. He makes his Christianity not just his religion, but his way of life, and trusts that God is preparing a room for him in heaven. I'm inexpressibly grateful to be "Papa's Punkin" (the nickname he's called me since I was born), and I want to follow his example. (Emma Miller)

My papa means so much to me. He has taught me so many great things about God and just things in life. I love him so much, and I love spending time with him. He is one of the most inspiring people in my life. This past year has been hard for me, but my papa knows just what to say. He told me that I don't need to care what people think about me, and what is important is that I believe that God will always help me and get me through tough times. He always knows how to encourage people, including me, and he is one of the wisest people I know in the Bible and just in life. When I grow up I want to be just like him. My papa is AMAZING and I love him so much. (Caleb Miller)

In my short years, my papa has taught me a lot about how to love people in a great big way. He has shown me how to have a lot of love for the people around me. Next week my best friend is moving to San Francisco, California.

This has made me sad and I've cried a lot because I'm going to miss her so much. I was telling my mom that I wished we had never met because now it makes her leaving so much harder because I love her so much. But I know that the sadness is worth it, because our friendship is so special and my heart is bigger to love. My papa has taught me to love with my whole heart. Sometimes when things are hard and people leave it can make me very sad, but my papa has shown me that loving people in a big way is always worth it. (Lexi Miller)

We're putting a lot of effort and planning to go see Papa in Boston these days. Because he can't walk, he can't come down to see us in Connecticut, so we go up there. It is probably easy for him to feel like, "Hey guys, I can't walk! Can you help me?" and to just be selfish. But instead, he decides to think about us and not himself. Although it's hard, he pulls through and never gives up. Even though he can't walk, he still walks with Jesus and always does the right thing. Even though he can't do much we still can do a lot with him. He reminds me of the scripture in Philippians 2:3–4: "Do nothing out of selfish ambition or vain conceit. Rather, in humility value others above yourselves, not looking to your own interests but each of you to the interests of the others." That is exactly what Papa does. And I love watching the Red Sox with him. (Micah Gonet)

FOR REFLECTION

No matter your age, think of what you want to leave as your legacy. Write these things down so that you can reflect on them periodically. How might your thoughts and actions today contribute to that legacy?

Wisdom Passes the Torch

Father, I thank you that Jesus showed us you so that we might know the way to live and think. Thank you for your word that instructs, sustains, comforts, and teaches us. I ask that you empower me to live my life each day so that the sum of my days will leave a legacy that helps those whose lives I touch to see you more clearly. Help me begin this legacy today. I long to pass on the things you teach me so that I can be both a learner and a teacher. In Jesus' name, Amen

54

WISDOM FINDS HOPE

Hope means everything to me. Without hope, I have nothing...really. As 1 Corinthians 15:19 (MSG) states:

> If all we get out of Christ is a little inspiration for a few short years, we're a pretty sorry lot.

Life in Christ is so much more than this. The passage continues:

> But the truth is that Christ has been raised up, the first in a long legacy of those who are going to leave the cemeteries.
>
> There is a nice symmetry in this: Death initially came by a man, and resurrection from death came by a man. Everybody dies in Adam; everybody comes alive in Christ. But we have to wait our turn: Christ is first, then those with him at his Coming, the grand consummation when, after crushing the opposition, he hands over his kingdom to God the Father. He won't let up until the last enemy is down—and the very last enemy is death! (1 Corinthians 15:20–26 MSG)

Physically, Wyndham can no longer do anything, really...except to love, to have faith, and to hope. Which really is everything that matters. Wisdom finds hope.

During times of suffering, I realize more keenly than ever the inexpressible blessing of hope. This world is not

Wisdom Finds Hope

what we are living for. Our lives, even if we live to old age, are a mist. The beauty, as Christians, is that we never have to say "goodbye," to each other, only "see you later." Because Jesus overcame death, the very last enemy, we have hope.

Wyndham's illness is a poignant reminder of our mortality. I believe that God works through our suffering. As we are emptied of all we have known together, we somehow see God more clearly, witnessing his power, love, and glory. Through this, we learn a deeper meaning of hope as expressed in Ephesians 1:18–19:

> I pray also that the eyes of your heart may be enlightened in order that you may know the hope to which he has called you, the riches of his glorious inheritance in the saints, and his incomparably great power for us who believe. That power is like the working of his mighty strength.

We have this hope because of one reason...because Jesus was raised so that we can be raised with him. We were raised with him when we were baptized into Christ; me in 1967, and Wyndham in 1972, overcoming the power of death and being raised into new, eternal life.

> We were therefore buried with him through baptism into death in order that, just as Christ was raised from the dead through the glory of the Father, we too may live a new life. (Romans 6:4)

I long to reach the point where I don't fear physical death...for there is no fear in love (1 John 4:18). I long to think as my granddaughter, Emery, inquired of her dad after a difficult weekend several months ago when we thought we were losing Wyndham. She asked, "Why would we be so sad with what you have told me about heaven? Shouldn't we be so happy for him?"

Yes, Emery, you are right. I suppose it is because we are mortal and can't see fully as God does (or perhaps as little children see). We struggle with this because we are human. Jesus understands; he grieved death as a human and grieved with those who lost loved ones. Years ago I heard an analogy that has helped me with this dilemma.

> If a baby in the womb could recount its thoughts, it would likely want to stay in the womb rather than enter some unknown world. Everything that it needs is in the womb. All feels good, even if it feels a bit cramped at times.
>
> But then comes the time to be born. If the unborn baby were told, "Proceed through this tiny, dark and uncomfortable passageway into a place you have never gone or seen" the response would likely be a kind, "No thank you" or a loudly screamed, "Not in a million years!"
>
> Unknown to this unborn child is what lies on the other side—a loving father's arms longing to receive his child saying, "You are so loved and you have no idea what is on this other side of life. You will find pizza, ice cream…and so much more. And arms that love and hold you…because you are mine."

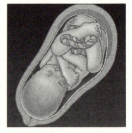

This is our hope—if we could only see. Heaven is so far beyond anything we can imagine, and God is waiting to receive us with arms that love and will hold us, because

Wisdom Finds Hope

we are his. We have been born into that living hope through the resurrection of Jesus (1 Peter 1:3–4).

Everything physical will perish, spoil, or fade. Our health one day will fail, and things we are tempted to place security in will be gone. But not eternal life, our gift from God. Nothing can take this from me. In Acts 2:24–26 Luke recounts David's words in Psalm 16:

> But God untied the death ropes and raised him up. Death was no match for him. David said it all:
>
> I saw God before me for all time.
>   Nothing can shake me; he's right by my side.
> I'm glad from the inside out, ecstatic;
>   I've pitched my tent in the land of hope. (MSG)

These words are so true, and I feel their presence in my life. Because Jesus conquered death, I can be glad from the inside out. I have pitched my tent in the land of hope.

FOR REFLECTION

What does hope mean to you? It is helpful, at times, to reflect on our mortality and who or what we live for as shown by our time, money, and thoughts. Do these aspects of your life reflect your hope of eternity? Are you placing your treasures in heaven where nothing can destroy them? If not, what one thing will you commit to change to enable you to focus on what truly matters the most?

Thank you, Jesus, for experiencing and conquering death so that I can live eternally. Father of all hope, help me, like David, to see you before me all the time and because of this to never be shaken. I place my time, my thoughts, my talents, my money, and my everything before you...knowing that you show me through your

WEDNESDAYS WITH WYNDHAM

word and your Spirit what is truly lasting and impor-
tant. Help me to live each day in a way to reflect your
glory. I place my hope in you, and for this, I am so
grateful. You are fully trustworthy and loving. In Jesus'
name, Amen.

55

WISDOM
Finishes Victoriously

Though I knew the day would come, I always longed for *the* day to be another day, not this one. But the day came. I said goodbye (for now) to my beloved Wyndham on November 21, 2019. I am grateful for every day and every extra day that God gave us. Two days before he died, I got to hear Wyndham's voice again, loud and clear. He told me clearly that he was going to die and that he loved me. We exchanged precious words of love. I assured him he would live on in me and in us, and I would love him forever. I tried to find some way to thank him for his love and his life. I reassured him we would be okay. This special time was a gift.

The next day he could not eat and was exceedingly tired, with a fever. His nurse thought he could possibly rebound, since he had in March, but that we would know in a few days. That night, Leigh Ann brought the three little

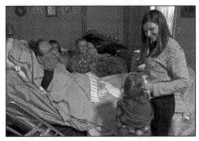

Shaw girls over to hug Papa, at Emery's insistence. Sam was out of town on a business trip. The girls beautifully sang for him, "Amazing Grace," "Twinkle Twinkle Little

Star," "Jesus Loves Me," and "He's Got the Whole World in His Hands," the last song with verses including every member of our family, including all the dogs. This was a gift that comforted him and brought him joy on what we did not know would be his last evening on earth. Later that night, Melissa, Kevin, and Kristen arrived, and we talked to him and prayed, cried, and laughed. Wyndham seemed to enjoy listening, though he could not respond except to squeeze his eyes. Sam made arrangements to fly back.

The next morning, Sam arrived and we all sat with Wyndham, unsure of what to expect. We sat with him and loved him with all that was within us. I had begged God that morning to be kind to Wyndham and to us in his passing, and he was. Wyndham was not in pain and the transition was fast. Our hearts broke for us but rejoiced for him as he exited this world with impeccable courage, gratitude, faith, and love. I could even see some cheerfulness before he passed, as his eyes smiled. I know that eye-smile. Since we still thought there was more time, I made a run to the drugstore to get a needed medical supply, and Kristen and Sam went for a prayer walk. Melissa and Kevin stayed with him. Jacob was nearby, attentive to the needs. As a family, we have been on this journey together, all in.

As soon as I walked out the door, Wyndham was gone, likely thinking of protecting me, once again. When I walked to him it was clear his body was vacant, a mere shell that once housed the spiritual being that still lives. For this certain hope, I give thanks to God.

The world felt a little dizzying that day and the next several days. The tears kept flowing, though accompanied by smiles and precious memories. I feel strangely both sad and grateful. It feels weird to be able to just walk out my door

Wisdom Finishes Victoriously

to go somewhere, and I find myself feeling guilty for being able to do so. That probably makes little sense, but many things feel a little strange right now. Transitions are hard. That dreaded day also brought many precious, touching moments, which are ours to treasure. There were also some moments that one day will give us laughter, but not yet.

The following day, when the hospital bed and medical equipment were all gone, our dog, Denver, walked into our room and just stood there as if frozen, looking around as if he were thinking, "Everything is different. What do I do now?" I felt the same.

Some of the grandchildren struggled while watching Wyndham's "things" go out the door. Wheelchairs and machines were familiar to the youngest ones and were connected to their papa. Sam reassured them that we were not taking Papa out of the house, but just the "sick" out of the house. Papa will always be with us because of all he gave us. For me, I look forward to the memories of pre-sick Wyndham returning, as I know they will. The last five of our forty-five years feel currently at the forefront, though I know that will change over time. These years are, however, sacred and precious, terribly hard though they were. We all grew and were changed, and our love only grew stronger. I have a keener sense of what is most important: Love God wholeheartedly. Love each other wholeheartedly and help as many as possible to know God. One. Day. At. A. Time.

When Wyndham received his diagnosis of the horrible disease called multiple system atrophy, we had a sobering idea of what could happen to his body, though it felt like a bad dream. Considering what was likely in store for his future, he studied the book of Job and committed to being grateful, faithful, courageous, and cheerful every day throughout his illness. He excelled in fulfilling this commitment to his last breath, even finding a way to laugh almost every day. Not one time did he complain or ask "Why me?" Instead, he felt, "Why not me?" I often tried to discourse with God on why such a good man had to suffer in such a drastic way. God did not tell me why, but we have all grown and changed because of this time. God didn't change the outcome, but he did change me. As much as I hate this disease, God has walked with us through it all, and he has been enough. For this I am grateful.

It does me no good to ask why, though truthfully I often have. If I could understand all of God's ways and how he sees beyond and works for good despite the evil in our fallen world, he would not be God, for God is beyond the dimension of human understanding. There is nothing I can do about that except to surrender and trust. He is God and I am not. He remains a good, good God, with a perspective that is beyond my reach. I know and believe God will continue to work in amazing ways as a result of Wyndham's life. I will thrill to witness ways God continues to work through the life Wyndham lived on earth. I am thankful for every moment that God gave me with Wyndham. Paul expresses this well:

> Every time I say your name in prayer—which is practically all the time—I thank God for you, the God I worship with my whole life in the tradition of my ancestors. I miss you a lot, especially when I remember that last tearful good-bye, and I look forward to a joy-packed reunion.
> That precious memory triggers another: your honest faith—and what a rich faith it is.
> (2 Timothy 1:3–5 MSG)

Wisdom Finishes Victoriously

Wyndham is no longer suffering, which makes me very happy for him. He fought the good fight and finished the race, and there is a great reward for him. I wish I could know what goes on in Paradise, but Paul himself said it cannot be stated (2 Corinthians 12:2–4). But Paul also says that the eternal glory makes the worst suffering seem like light and momentary trouble. Only someday will I understand this.

I miss Wyndham more than words can express and am forever grateful he has shown me the wisdom of how to live and to die in the Lord...with a pure heart, a good conscience, and a sincere faith (1 Timothy 1:5).

I know Wyndham would pass these words on today:

> But you—keep your eye on what you're doing; accept the hard times along with the good; keep the Message alive; do a thorough job as God's servant.
>
> You take over. I'm about to die, my life an offering on God's altar.
>
> This is the only race worth running. I've run hard right to the finish, believed all the way. All that's left now is the shouting—God's applause! Depend on it, he's an honest judge. He'll do right not only by me, but by everyone eager for his coming.
> (2 Timothy 4:5–8 MSG)

FOR REFLECTION

Reflect on the meaning of eternity, even though it is beyond our comprehension. Determine where you

are storing your treasures. How might you better prepare for eternal life? Is your concept of heaven such that the most wonderful thing about it is God's presence? If not, how might you grow in your love for and relationship with him?

Father, please open my eyes that I might understand what is truly important in life. I long to seek your face above everything else, so that I can truly know eternal life—relationship with you. I want to make choices that strengthen my relationship with you, rather than weaken it. Give me wisdom, discernment, and love to choose you above everything else. Thank you, Jesus, that you defeated death, so I can have hope, real hope. I love you and long to be in your presence, but while here I want to help populate heaven. Because of Jesus, Amen.

56

WISDOM
WRITES NEW CHAPTERS

I try to imagine Wyndham's thrill as he enjoys his new chapter of life in Paradise. As the Scriptures speak concerning wisdom:

> Yet among the mature we do speak wisdom, though it is not a wisdom of this age or of the rulers of this age, who are doomed to perish. But we speak God's wisdom, secret and hidden, which God decreed before the ages for our glory. None of the rulers of this age understood this; for if they had, they would not have crucified the Lord of glory.
>
> But, as it is written,
>
> "What no eye has seen, nor ear heard,
>   nor the human heart conceived,
> what God has prepared for those who love him"
> (1 Corinthians 2:6–9 NRSV)

As I read these verses, I realize that this wisdom and these promises are not just for those who are no longer living here physically. They are for you and me. Now. As I live my life with God, I will understand more of what God has prepared for me in these next chapters. I loved the previous chapters, hard though the last several were, and wait in expectation for God to work in new ones.

I reluctantly must turn the pages of my life to find the new, unwritten-on pages. Every new day God gives us is an opportunity to write a new chapter. One. Word. At. A. Time. I felt I would never be ready to start this new chapter in life, but God obviously thinks differently than I. He must believe that I am ready. My emotions war within, often feeling it is not fair to enjoy life when Wyndham was so trapped in his body. He and I had operated in partnership for forty-five years, yet in ways, I realize that some form of partnership will always exist as he remains with me in heart and memory. If the tables were turned, and I was the one who first departed the earth, I would long for him to enjoy the good things God gives in this life. I know he wishes this for me. I also understand, because I am still here and have not yet been called home, that God is not finished with me yet. Nor is he with you. I pray to be a noble vessel God can use to bring glory to him.

I stand amazed at some of the conversations and remarks that have come from both Wyndham's life and death. They bring me to my knees in awe of God at work. God is still working through Wyndham's life and will continue to do so.

I don't know what life holds in store for me, but I commit to living each day as Wyndham so valiantly chose to do—with faith, courage, gratitude, and cheerfulness. One day at a time. With God. I am finding that gratitude and giving are the most important healing salves for my heart. Thank you for sharing this journey with me, and with us. As I think of the awaiting chapters in my life, C.S. Lewis puts my imagination to words as he closes *The Chronicles of Narnia:*

Wisdom Writes New Chapters

The things that began to happen after that were so great and beautiful that I cannot write them. And for us this is the end of all the stories, and we can most truly say that they all lived happily ever after. But for them it was only the beginning of the real story. All their life in this world and all their adventures in Narnia had only been the cover and the title page: now at last they were beginning Chapter One of the Great Story, which no one on earth has read: which goes on forever: in which every chapter is better than the one before.[4]

We will each write the story of our lives every day God gives us. While the pages ahead are blank, we will put words on them and let God edit them. May we begin today to write the stories of God's wisdom in our lives so that one day we will be with him, experiencing the unimaginable and glorious plan made available for you and me.

No, the wisdom we speak of is the mystery of God—his plan that was previously hidden, even though he made it for our ultimate glory before the world began. But the rulers of this world have not understood it; if they had, they would not have crucified our glorious Lord.
That is what the Scriptures mean when they say,

"No eye has seen, no ear has heard,
and no mind has imagined
what God has prepared
for those who love him."

But it was to us that God revealed these things by his Spirit. For his Spirit searches out everything and shows us God's deep secrets.
(1 Corinthians 2:7–10 NLT)

---

4. C.S. Lewis, *The Last Battle* (New York: Collier, 1970), 183–184.

For Reflection

Do you get overwhelmed with "activities" of life so that you find little time to be still with God? Consider that this kind of busyness will only change by you making intentional, even radical decisions to spend needed time praying, meditating, and reading the Bible, drawing close to God. Consider taking a spiritual retreat for several hours with just you and God. Think through your core values and how your lifestyle can better match a decision to put God first, one day at a time, every day.

> *Father, nothing is more important to me than my relationship with you. Help me recognize and clear any hindrances to our relationship so that you will be my first and greatest love. As I begin writing the unwritten pages of my life, I long to surrender to your will, trusting you and bringing glory to you all my days, until I see you face to face. In Jesus' name, Amen.*

Made in the USA
Middletown, DE
07 December 2020